Becoming A

FATHER

Embracing Your Roles With Grace and Strength

Bisi & Toyin Tofade

Becoming A Godly Father

Table Of Contents

Chapter 1: Embracing the Roles of a Godly Father   3

Chapter 2: The 7 P's of a Godly Father   23

Chapter 3: Fatherhood and Discipline   37

Chapter 4: Fatherhood and Teaching Values and Morals   42

Chapter 5: Fatherhood and Serving as a Role Model   52

Chapter 6: Abusive Fathers   66

Embracing Your Roles With Grace and Strength

Becoming A Godly Father

Chapter 7: Reconciliation and Renewal: Fathers in Conflict with Their Children   89

Chapter 8: Family and Relationships   102

Embracing Your Roles With Grace and Strength

Chapter 1: Embracing the Roles of a Godly Father

Different kinds of Fathers

In our society today, we see a diverse spectrum of fathers, each impacting their families and communities in different ways. There are fathers who exemplify the best qualities of leadership and responsibility, creating nurturing and supportive environments for their families.

Conversely, there are fathers whose actions and behaviors contribute to familial discord and instability. Some fathers serve as inspiring role models, guiding their children with wisdom and integrity, while others fall short, failing to provide the positive examples their children need.

Ephesians 6:4 (KJV)

And, ye fathers, provoke not your children to wrath: but bring them up in the nurture and admonition of the Lord.

Colossians 3:21 (KJV)

Fathers, provoke not your children to anger, lest they be discouraged.

Let's take a closer look at the various kinds of fathers found in our society:

Becoming a Godly Father

1. Responsible Fathers (Nurturing Fathers):

Responsible fathers are actively involved in their children's lives and prioritize their well-being. They provide emotional support, guidance, and discipline to their children.

Responsible fathers take an active role in their children's education, extracurricular activities, and personal development. They prioritize spending quality time with their children and are present for important milestones and events in their lives.

2. Irresponsible (Neglectful) Fathers:

Irresponsible fathers may neglect their parental duties and fail to provide emotional or financial support to their children. They may struggle with addiction, mental health issues, or other personal challenges that prevent them from being present and engaged in their children's lives.

Irresponsible fathers may exhibit inconsistent or harmful behavior that negatively impacts their children's well-being. They may be emotionally distant, physically absent, or indifferent to their children's well-being.

Neglectful fathers often prioritize their own needs or interests over those of their children, leading to feelings of abandonment and neglect.

3. Careless Fathers:

Careless fathers may be physically present but emotionally distant from their children. They may fail to understand or meet their children's emotional needs or provide adequate support and guidance.

Careless fathers may prioritize work, hobbies, or other interests over their children, leading to feelings of neglect or abandonment. They may exhibit a lack of interest or investment in their children's lives, resulting in strained or distant relationships.

4. Absentee Fathers:

Absentee fathers are largely or completely absent from their children's lives, either physically or emotionally. They may have little to no contact with their children, leading to feelings of abandonment and loss.

Absentee fathers may be estranged from their children due to factors such as divorce, death, separation, incarceration, or personal issues. Their absence can have long-lasting impacts on their children's emotional well-being, self-esteem, and relationships with others.

Becoming a Godly Father

5. Abusive Fathers:

Abusive fathers engage in harmful and destructive behavior towards their children, including physical, emotional, or verbal abuse. They may use power and control tactics to intimidate, manipulate, or harm their children, creating an environment of fear and insecurity.

Abusive fathers may exhibit controlling or violent behavior that causes lasting trauma and harm to their children. It is important to seek help and support in situations of abuse to protect the well-being and safety of both the children and the parent.

6. Enabling (Permissive) Fathers:

Enabling fathers may shield their children from facing the consequences of their actions or behavior, hindering their personal growth and accountability. They may prioritize keeping the peace or avoiding conflict, even at the expense of their children's development and well-being. Enabling fathers may fail to set appropriate boundaries or provide guidance and discipline, leading to a lack of responsibility and maturity in their children.

It is important for fathers to strike a balance between support and accountability in order to promote healthy growth and development in their children.

Becoming a Godly Father

Permissive fathers are lenient and often avoid setting boundaries. They may prioritize their children's happiness in the short term, but this lack of structure can lead to behavioral issues and difficulty in managing responsibilities and expectations.

Some other types of fathers include spiritual fathers where the main linkage is due to a religious connection that created a fatherly bond. This "fatherhood" is not defined by chronological age but spiritual experience and wisdom in matters of faith.

An adoptive Father is one who has the connection through a legal process of transfer from the birth parent to the adoptive parent. Typically, forms are completed and signed to make this official.

A God father is typically identified during the birth or baptismal process of a child. This individual is usually assigned by the birth parents as a person they trust deeply, who will watch over the progress of the child through life. Depending on the relationship building process, this could end up being very positive or just in name only.

Step fathers are usually a father figure available to a child because a parent remarried. This relationship could range from being involved and positive, uninvolved or involved and negative.

Becoming a Godly Father

Understanding the different types of fathers in society highlights the varied impacts paternal figures can have on their families. While some fathers uplift and inspire, others may falter and fail. Recognizing these differences allows us to appreciate the importance of positive fatherhood and the profound effect it has on shaping well-rounded, emotionally healthy individuals. Fathers who strive to lead with love, consistency, and integrity set a powerful foundation for their children's futures, fostering a healthier and more stable society.

Understanding the Importance of Fatherhood

Fatherhood is a crucial role that men have the opportunity to embrace with grace and strength. Understanding the importance of fatherhood is essential in order to fulfill this role effectively. Fathers play a significant role in shaping the lives of their children and families, and their presence and influence are invaluable. By understanding the significance of fatherhood, men can better appreciate the impact they have on their children and families.

One of the key aspects of understanding the importance of fatherhood is recognizing the role that fathers play in shaping the values and morals of their children. Fathers have the opportunity to instill important values such as honesty, integrity, and respect in their children. By modeling these values in their own lives and teaching them to their children, fathers can help guide their children on the path to becoming responsible and upstanding individuals.

Becoming a Godly Father

Fatherhood also involves providing discipline and guidance to children in order to help them develop into well-rounded individuals. Discipline is an important aspect of parenting that helps children learn right from wrong and develop self-control. Fathers can provide discipline in a loving and consistent manner, setting boundaries and expectations for their children while also offering guidance and support. By understanding the importance of discipline in fatherhood, men can help their children grow and thrive in a healthy and structured environment.

Another important aspect of understanding the importance of fatherhood is serving as a role model for children. Fathers have a unique opportunity to demonstrate positive behaviors and traits for their children to emulate. By being present, involved, and supportive in their children's lives, fathers can show them what it means to be a responsible and caring individual. Fathers who serve as positive role models can have a lasting impact on their children, helping them develop into confident and compassionate adults.

The negative impact in the society of absence of fathers in the lives of their children

The absence of fathers in the lives of their children has significant negative impacts on society. This phenomenon, often resulting from divorce, separation, or extra-marital births, can lead to a range of adverse outcomes for children, families, and the broader community. These impacts are multifaceted, affecting emotional, social, and economic dimensions. When fathers are missing, many things are lost in the lives of the children.

Embracing Your Roles With Grace and Strength

Becoming a Godly Father

Scripture Example

Zecharias: The Father of John The Baptist. Luke 1:57-64 (KJV)

Although Zecharias, the father, was present at the time of naming his son, he was unable to speak. As a result, neighbors and cousins attempted to take over his role as head of the family, nearly succeeding in naming the child Zecharias Jr., contrary to the angel's revelation.

This situation highlights the crucial importance of fathers playing their roles in the family. When a father is absent or merely a figurehead, others —such as cousins, uncles, and neighbors—may assume his responsibilities. Consequently, the mother is burdened with decision-making and disciplinary duties.

Here are some of the negative effects of a father's absence in the lives of his children:

Becoming a Godly Father

Emotional and Psychological Effects

1. **Emotional Instability**: Children without a father figure often experience emotional instability. They may struggle with feelings of abandonment, low self-esteem, and insecurity. This emotional turmoil can lead to behavioral problems, depression, and anxiety.
2. **Identity Issues**: Fathers play a crucial role in shaping their children's sense of identity. Their absence can lead to difficulties in self-identity, particularly in adolescents, who may struggle to find their place in society.
3. **Attachment Problems**: The lack of a father figure can result in poor attachment, impacting the child's ability to form healthy relationships in the future. This can lead to trust issues and problems in forming intimate relationships.

Reference: National Institute of health/National Library of Medicine
https://www.ncbi.nlm.nih.gov/pmc/articles/PMC3904543/

Becoming a Godly Father

Social and Behavioral Consequences

1. **Increased Risk of Delinquency**: Studies have shown that children from father-absent homes are more likely to engage in criminal behavior and substance abuse. The lack of paternal guidance and supervision can contribute to these outcomes.
2. **Educational Challenges**: Fatherless children often face academic challenges, including lower academic performance and higher dropout rates. Fathers often provide support and motivation for academic achievement, and their absence can negatively affect a child's educational trajectory.
3. **Socialization Issues**: The absence of a father can hinder a child's social development. Children may have difficulty interacting with peers and authority figures, which can affect their social competence and integration.

Economic Impact

1. **Economic Hardship**: Single-parent households, particularly those headed by mothers, are more likely to experience economic hardship. This can lead to a lower standard of living, limited access to resources, and increased stress for both the parent and the child.
2. **Cycle of Poverty**: The economic disadvantages faced by single-parent households can perpetuate a cycle of poverty. Children growing up in such environments are less likely to have access to educational and extracurricular opportunities, which can limit their future earning potential.

Reference: Minnesota Psychological Association -(Bronte-Tinkew, Jacinta, Moore, Capps, & Zaff, 2004)
https://www.mnpsych.org/index.php

Becoming a Godly Father

Broader Societal Implications

1. **Strain on Social Services**: The issues faced by fatherless children can lead to an increased reliance on social services, including mental health services, juvenile justice systems, and financial assistance programs. This can strain public resources and increase government spending.
2. **Community Stability**: High rates of father absence can contribute to community instability. Neighborhoods with a high prevalence of single-parent families may experience higher crime rates, lower property values, and a reduced sense of community cohesion.
3. **Generational Impact**: The absence of fathers can have a generational impact, as children who grow up without a father figure are more likely to become single parents themselves. This perpetuates a cycle of father absence and its associated negative consequences.

Mitigating the Impact

Addressing the negative impact of father absence requires comprehensive strategies, including:

Becoming a Godly Father

1. **Supporting Single Mothers**: Providing economic, emotional, and social support to single mothers can help mitigate the adverse effects on children. This includes access to affordable childcare, job training, and mental health services.
2. **Encouraging Father Involvement**: Promoting policies and programs that encourage and facilitate father involvement, even in cases of divorce or separation, can help maintain a paternal presence in children's lives.
3. **Community Programs**: Implementing community-based programs that provide mentorship and support for fatherless children can offer positive male role models and guidance.
4. **Education and Awareness**: Raising awareness about the importance of father involvement and educating parents about co-parenting strategies can help reduce the incidence of father absence.

Becoming a Godly Father

In conclusion, understanding the importance of fatherhood is essential for men who are embracing the role of being a godly father. By recognizing the significance of fatherhood in shaping the lives of children and families, men can fulfill their role with grace and strength. Embracing the roles of a godly father, providing discipline, teaching values and morals, and serving as a role model are all essential aspects of fatherhood that men should strive to embody.

By understanding and embracing these aspects of fatherhood, men can make a positive impact on their children and families and contribute to the well-being and growth of future generations.

Embracing the Responsibilities of Fatherhood

Embracing the Responsibilities of Fatherhood is a crucial aspect of being a godly father. As men and fathers, it is important to understand the weight of our role and the impact it has on our children and families. Fatherhood is not just about providing for our families financially, but also emotionally, spiritually, and mentally. It is about being present and actively involved in the lives of our children, guiding them with grace and strength.

Becoming a Godly Father

One of the key responsibilities of fatherhood is discipline. Discipline is not about punishment, but about teaching and guiding our children towards becoming responsible and respectful individuals. As godly fathers, we must set boundaries and enforce consequences when necessary, while also showing love and understanding. By instilling discipline in our children, we are helping them develop self-control, respect for authority, and a strong work ethic.

Another important aspect of fatherhood is teaching values and morals. As fathers, we have the opportunity to shape the character and integrity of our children by imparting values such as honesty, empathy, and compassion. By leading by example and living out these values in our own lives, we are teaching our children the importance of integrity and virtue. It is essential to have open and honest conversations with our children about what is right and wrong, and to help them navigate the complexities of the world with a strong moral compass.

Fatherhood also involves serving as a role model for our children. Our actions speak louder than words, and as fathers, we must strive to embody the qualities and characteristics we want to see in our children. By demonstrating kindness, patience, and humility, we are showing our children what it means to be a godly father. Serving as a positive role model also means being present and engaged in our children's lives, participating in their activities, and showing them love and support in all that they do.

Embracing Your Roles With Grace and Strength

Becoming a Godly Father

The Sons of Rechab: A Classical example of the Influence of a Father

In Jeremiah 35:1-8, the story of the sons of Rechab offers profound lessons about the role of a father as an instructor and role model in the lives of their children. Jonadab, the forefather of the Rechabites, provided his descendants with specific instructions about how to live, which they faithfully followed for generations. This narrative highlights several key aspects of paternal influence and the lasting impact of a father's guidance and example.

Consistency in Instruction

Jonadab's instructions to his children were clear and consistent. He commanded them not to drink wine, build houses, sow seed, or plant vineyards, but to live in tents all their days. This consistent and unwavering set of rules helped the Rechabites develop a strong sense of identity and purpose. A father's role as an instructor involves setting clear, consistent guidelines and expectations for behavior and lifestyle. When these instructions are communicated effectively, they provide a stable foundation upon which children can build their lives.

Becoming a Godly Father

Legacy of Obedience

The Rechabites' obedience to Jonadab's commands illustrates the power of a father's influence across generations. Despite the passage of time and changing circumstances, the descendants of Jonadab adhered to his directives.

This obedience highlights the deep respect and trust they had in their father's wisdom. Fathers who act as instructors not only impact their immediate children but also set a precedent for future generations, fostering a culture of respect and adherence to family values and principles.

Role Modeling

Jonadab didn't just give instructions; he lived by them. His lifestyle and choices served as a living example for his descendants. A father's actions often speak louder than his words. By embodying the values and behaviors he wishes to instill in his children, a father acts as a powerful role model. Children learn by observing their parents, and a father who lives according to his own teachings reinforces those lessons through his example.

Embracing Your Roles With Grace and Strength

Becoming a Godly Father

Strength in Unity

The Rechabites demonstrated a strong sense of community and unity, which was directly tied to their adherence to Jonadab's instructions. This unity provided them with resilience and strength, particularly in times of challenge. A father's role includes fostering a sense of belonging and unity within the family. By teaching children to value their family heritage and support one another, a father helps build a cohesive and resilient family unit.

Moral and Ethical Guidance

Jonadab's commands were not arbitrary; they were designed to keep his descendants morally and ethically grounded. By avoiding wine and a settled, agricultural lifestyle, the Rechabites maintained a level of purity and simplicity that set them apart. Fathers provide crucial moral and ethical guidance, helping their children navigate the complexities of life with integrity and wisdom. This guidance helps children develop a strong moral compass and make decisions that align with their family values.

Adaptability and Resilience

The Rechabites' ability to adhere to Jonadab's instructions, even when offered wine by the prophet Jeremiah in a setting that could have easily led to compromise, demonstrates remarkable resilience and adaptability.

Becoming a Godly Father

Fathers who instill a strong sense of identity and purpose in their children equip them to withstand external pressures and remain true to their values in diverse situations.

The Importance of Spiritual Leadership

Jonadab's instructions had a spiritual dimension, as they were likely influenced by a desire to remain faithful to God's commands and avoid the corrupt practices of surrounding nations. Fathers play a critical role in the spiritual development of their children, guiding them in faith practices and helping them understand and live by spiritual principles.

Conclusion

The story of the sons of Rechab in Jeremiah 35:1-8 provides rich lessons on the role of a father as an instructor and role model. Fathers have a profound impact on their children's lives through consistent instruction, exemplary living, fostering unity, providing moral and ethical guidance, and leading spiritually. By embracing these roles, fathers can ensure their legacy endures, guiding their children and future generations toward a life of integrity, resilience, and faithfulness.

Becoming a Godly Father

Embracing the responsibilities of fatherhood is a sacred and noble calling. As men and fathers, we have the power to positively influence the lives of our children and families by being present, loving, and intentional in our actions. By embracing our role with grace and strength, we can raise children who are respectful, responsible, and compassionate individuals. Let us strive to be godly fathers who lead by example, teach values and morals, and serve as role models for our children and future generations.

Cultivating a Strong Relationship with Your Children

Cultivating a strong relationship with your children is essential in being a godly father. As men and fathers, it is our responsibility to nurture and build a bond with our children that will last a lifetime. This subchapter will explore the importance of this relationship and provide practical tips on how to strengthen it.

Fatherhood is a sacred role that requires love, patience, and understanding. By embracing this role with grace and strength, we can set a positive example for our children and help them grow into responsible, compassionate adults. Building a strong relationship with our children starts with spending quality time with them, listening to their thoughts and feelings, and showing them unconditional love and support.

Chapter 2: The 7 P's of a Godly Father

1. Presence

A good father is present in his children's lives both physically and emotionally. He takes an active interest in their activities, listens to them, and makes time to be with them.

In the journey of becoming a godly father, one of the key aspects to focus on is presence. A good father is not only physically present in his children's lives, but also emotionally available. This means actively participating in their activities, listening to their thoughts and feelings, and making time to spend quality moments together. Being present in a child's life is crucial for building a strong bond and nurturing a healthy relationship.

When a father is present in his children's lives, he shows them that they are valued and loved. By taking an active interest in their activities, whether it's attending their sports games, school events, or simply playing with them at home, a father demonstrates his commitment to being there for his children. This presence helps children feel secure, supported, and understood, which are essential for their emotional development and well-being.

Becoming a Godly Father

Listening to children is another important aspect of being a present father. By truly hearing and understanding their thoughts, feelings, and concerns, a father can build trust and open communication with his children. This allows for meaningful conversations, problem-solving, and emotional support that can strengthen the parent-child relationship. Being a good listener shows children that their father cares about them and is there to support them through life's challenges.

Making time to be with children is a priority for a good father. Despite busy schedules and responsibilities, finding moments to spend quality time with each child individually and as a family is essential for creating lasting memories and connections. Whether it's reading bedtime stories, going on outings, or having family dinners, these shared experiences help build a sense of unity and belonging within the family. Being present in these moments creates a sense of togetherness and reinforces the father's role as a supportive and loving figure in his children's lives.

Presence is a foundational aspect of being a godly father. By being physically and emotionally present in their children's lives, fathers can nurture strong relationships, build trust and communication, and create lasting memories. Being present in a child's life shows love, support, and commitment, which are essential for their growth and development. Embracing the role of a present father is a meaningful and rewarding journey that can positively impact both the parent and child for years to come.

Embracing Your Roles With Grace and Strength

Becoming a Godly Father

2. Patience

A good father exhibits patience in dealing with his children, understanding that nurturing and guiding them through challenges takes time and effort. He remains calm in difficult situations and provides support when needed.

Patience is a key trait that every good father must possess when it comes to raising his children. In the journey of fatherhood, understanding that nurturing and guiding children through challenges takes time and effort is crucial. It is important for a father to remain calm in difficult situations and provide support when needed. Patience allows a father to navigate through the ups and downs of parenting with grace and strength.

As a father, it is essential to recognize that children are constantly learning and growing. It is normal for them to make mistakes and face challenges along the way. A good father exhibits patience by understanding that these experiences are opportunities for growth and development. By remaining patient, a father can guide his children through these challenges, teaching them valuable lessons along the way.

In difficult situations, a father's patience can make all the difference. By staying calm and composed, a father can provide a sense of stability and security for his children. This sense of support is essential for children to feel safe and cared for, even in the face of adversity. Patience allows a father to be a pillar of strength for his family, no matter what challenges come their way.

Becoming a Godly Father

Patience also plays a crucial role in teaching values and morals to children. By demonstrating patience in challenging moments, a father can model important virtues such as perseverance, empathy, and resilience. Children learn by example, and a patient father sets a positive and powerful example for his children to follow. Through patience, a father can instill core values that will guide his children throughout their lives.

In serving as a role model, a father's patience is a powerful tool. By exhibiting patience in his interactions with others, a father shows his children how to handle difficult situations with grace and strength. This example not only teaches children important life skills, but also fosters a sense of respect and admiration for their father. Patience is truly a cornerstone of godly fatherhood, allowing a father to lead by example and guide his children with love and understanding.

Becoming a Godly Father

3. Protection

A good father protects his children from harm, both physically and emotionally. He creates a safe and secure environment for them to grow and develop.

In the journey of becoming a godly father, one of the key responsibilities that must be embraced is that of protection. A good father understands the importance of creating a safe and secure environment for his children to grow and develop. This includes not only physical protection from harm, but also emotional protection from the challenges and difficulties of life. By being vigilant and proactive in safeguarding his children, a father demonstrates his love and commitment to their well-being.

Physically, a good father takes measures to protect his children from harm by ensuring their safety in all aspects of life. This may involve childproofing the home, teaching them about stranger danger, and supervising them during outdoor activities. By being present and attentive, a father can prevent accidents and keep his children out of harm's way. Additionally, a good father instills in his children the importance of self-care and responsibility for their own safety.

Becoming a Godly Father

Emotionally, a good father provides a nurturing and supportive environment for his children to thrive. He listens to their concerns, offers guidance and reassurance, and helps them navigate through the challenges of life. By being a source of strength and comfort, a father helps his children develop resilience and coping skills. This emotional protection is essential for fostering a strong bond between father and child, and for instilling a sense of security and trust in the relationship.

In serving as a role model for his children, a good father demonstrates the importance of protection by showing them how to be strong and compassionate. He leads by example, showing them how to stand up for themselves and others, how to be kind and empathetic, and how to prioritize their well-being. By embodying these qualities, a father teaches his children the value of protection and empowers them to take care of themselves and others.

Ultimately, protection is a foundational aspect of fatherhood that requires grace and strength. By embracing the role of protector, a good father demonstrates his love and commitment to his children, and helps them grow into confident and resilient individuals. Through his actions and words, a father can create a safe and secure environment for his children to thrive, and instill in them the values of protection and care.

Becoming a Godly Father

4. Provider

A good father provides for his children's needs, whether it be financial support, emotional support, or guidance. He ensures that his children have the resources they need to thrive.

In the journey of becoming a godly father, one of the most important roles you will embrace is that of a provider. A good father understands the importance of meeting his children's needs, whether they be financial, emotional, or guidance-related. Providing for your children goes beyond just putting food on the table and a roof over their heads. It means ensuring that they have the resources they need to thrive and succeed in all aspects of their lives.

Financial support is a crucial aspect of being a provider as a father. This means working hard to provide for your family and making sure that they have all the necessities they need to live comfortably. It also means teaching your children the value of hard work and responsibility when it comes to managing money. By being a good steward of your resources, you set a positive example for your children to follow in their own lives.

Becoming a Godly Father

Emotional support is another key element of being a provider as a father. Children need to feel loved, supported, and understood by their parents in order to thrive emotionally. A good father provides a safe and nurturing environment for his children to express themselves and seek comfort when needed. By being there for your children emotionally, you help them develop a strong sense of self-worth and confidence.

Guidance is also an essential aspect of being a provider as a father. Children look to their parents for guidance and direction as they navigate the ups and downs of life. A good father provides wise counsel and advice to his children, helping them make decisions that will benefit them in the long run. By being a source of guidance and support, you empower your children to make wise choices and grow into responsible adults.

In conclusion, being a provider as a father is a multifaceted role that involves meeting your children's needs in various ways. Whether it's financial support, emotional support, or guidance, a good father ensures that his children have the resources they need to thrive and succeed. By embracing the role of a provider, you set a positive example for your children to follow and help them grow into confident, responsible, and successful individuals.

Becoming a Godly Father

5. Playfulness

A good father knows the importance of having fun and spending quality time with his children. He engages in play and activities that foster bonding and create lasting memories.

As fathers, it is crucial to understand the significance of playfulness in our relationships with our children. Playfulness is not just about having fun; it is about building strong connections and creating lasting memories. A good father knows how to engage in activities that bring joy and laughter to his children's lives, fostering a sense of closeness and bonding that will last a lifetime.

Spending quality time with our children through play is essential for their emotional and social development. When we engage in activities that are enjoyable and stimulating, we are not only strengthening our relationship with them but also helping them to build confidence, creativity, and problem-solving skills. Playfulness creates a safe space for children to express themselves and explore their interests, making them feel loved and valued by their father.

Becoming a Godly Father

By being playful, fathers can also teach important life lessons and values to their children in a natural and engaging way. Through play, children learn about teamwork, communication, and sportsmanship, as well as empathy, kindness, and respect for others. A good father uses play as a tool to instill these values in his children, setting the foundation for them to become compassionate and responsible individuals in the future.

Furthermore, playfulness allows fathers to serve as positive role models for their children. When fathers are actively involved in play and activities with their children, they demonstrate the importance of spending time together and building strong relationships. Children look up to their fathers as guides and mentors, and by engaging in playful interactions, fathers show their children the joy and fulfillment that come from being present and involved in their lives.

Embracing playfulness as a father is essential for creating strong, loving, and meaningful relationships with our children. By engaging in fun and stimulating activities, we not only foster bonding and create lasting memories but also teach important life lessons and values. Playfulness is a powerful tool for fathers to serve as role models and guide their children towards becoming compassionate, responsible, and well-rounded individuals.

Becoming a Godly Father

6. Praise

A good father offers praise and encouragement to his children, recognizing their accomplishments and efforts. This helps build their self-esteem and confidence.

A good father offers praise and encouragement to his children, recognizing their accomplishments and efforts. By acknowledging their achievements, a father helps build their self-esteem and confidence, shaping them into individuals who believe in their own abilities.

Praise is not just about acknowledging success; it is also about recognizing the effort put forth by children. When a father praises his children for their hard work, determination, and perseverance, he instills in them a sense of pride and motivation to continue striving for excellence. This positive reinforcement can go a long way in shaping the character and work ethic of children, helping them develop into responsible and successful individuals.

Furthermore, offering praise and encouragement helps children feel valued and appreciated by their father. This sense of validation can strengthen the bond between father and child, creating a supportive and loving relationship based on mutual respect and admiration. When children feel seen and heard by their father, they are more likely to open up and share their thoughts and feelings, fostering a deeper connection and understanding.

Becoming a Godly Father

As fathers, it is important to be mindful of the impact our words and actions have on our children. By offering genuine praise and encouragement, we not only boost their self-esteem and confidence but also teach them the importance of recognizing and celebrating the achievements of others. This sets a positive example for children to follow, encouraging them to be kind, supportive, and encouraging towards their peers as well.

In conclusion, praise plays a crucial role in parenting and in shaping the character of children. A good father recognizes the accomplishments and efforts of his children, offering them praise and encouragement to build their self-esteem and confidence. By fostering a culture of appreciation and validation, fathers can strengthen their relationship with their children and help them develop into compassionate, confident, and successful individuals.

7. Positive Role Model

A good father serves as a positive role model for his children, demonstrating values such as honesty, integrity, respect, and responsibility. He sets an example for his children to follow and guides them in making good choices.

In the journey of becoming a godly father, one of the most important roles that a father plays is that of being a positive role model for his children. A good father serves as a shining example of honesty, integrity, respect, and responsibility, demonstrating these values in his daily actions and interactions.

Becoming a Godly Father

By embodying these qualities, a father sets a powerful example for his children to follow, guiding them in making good choices and shaping their character.

Children look up to their fathers as heroes and mentors, seeking guidance on how to navigate the complexities of life. A father who exemplifies positive values and behaviors not only teaches his children right from wrong, but also instills in them a strong moral compass that will guide them throughout their lives. By consistently modeling honesty, integrity, respect, and responsibility, a father helps his children develop a solid foundation of values that they can rely on as they grow and mature.

Furthermore, serving as a positive role model allows a father to build strong and lasting relationships with his children. When children see their father living out the values he teaches, they are more likely to trust and respect him. This trust and respect form the basis of a healthy and loving parent-child relationship, fostering open communication, mutual understanding, and a sense of security for the children.

As a father embraces the role of being a positive role model, he not only benefits his children, but also contributes to the well-being of society as a whole.

Becoming a Godly Father

Children who are raised by fathers who embody positive values are more likely to become responsible, compassionate, and productive members of society. By serving as a positive role model, a father can help shape the next generation of leaders, influencers, and change-makers who will make a positive impact on the world.

Being a positive role model is a crucial aspect of fatherhood that cannot be understated. A good father who demonstrates values such as honesty, integrity, respect, and responsibility sets a powerful example for his children to follow, guiding them in making good choices and shaping their character. By embracing the role of being a positive role model, fathers can build strong relationships with their children, instill strong values and morals, and contribute to the betterment of society as a whole.

Chapter 3: Fatherhood and Discipline

Setting Boundaries and Consistent Discipline

Setting boundaries and consistent discipline are essential components of being a godly father. As men and fathers, it is our responsibility to set clear expectations for our children and uphold those boundaries with love and consistency. By doing so, we are teaching our children respect, self-discipline, and the importance of following rules.

Discipline is not about punishment; it is about teaching and guiding our children towards making good choices. Consistent discipline helps children understand the consequences of their actions and encourages them to think before they act. As fathers, we must be firm but fair in our approach to discipline, always keeping in mind that our ultimate goal is to help our children grow into responsible, respectful adults.

> *If ye endure chastening, God dealeth with you as with sons; for what son is he whom the father chasteneth not? 8 But if ye be without chastisement, whereof all are partakers, then are ye bastards, and not sons. 9 Furthermore we have had fathers of our flesh which corrected us, and we gave them reverence: shall we not much rather be in subjection unto the Father of spirits, and live?*
>
> *Hebrews 12:7-9 KJV*

Becoming a Godly Father

Teaching values and morals is another crucial aspect of fatherhood. Our children look to us as their role models, so it is important that we lead by example and instill in them the values and morals that will guide them throughout their lives. Whether it is honesty, integrity, compassion, or perseverance, we must consistently model these traits and teach our children why they are important.

As fathers, we have a unique opportunity to shape the character and values of our children. By serving as a role model and embodying the qualities we wish to instill in our children, we are teaching them by example. Our actions speak louder than our words, so it is important that we strive to live out the values we want our children to uphold.

Teaching Discipline with Love and Understanding

Discipline is a crucial aspect of parenting, but it is often misunderstood as being solely about punishment and control. In reality, teaching discipline with love and understanding is about guiding and shaping a child's behavior in a positive way. As fathers, it is our responsibility to show our children that discipline is not about instilling fear, but about teaching them right from wrong with compassion and empathy.

Becoming a Godly Father

When it comes to discipline, it is important to set clear and consistent boundaries for our children. By establishing rules and consequences early on, we can help them understand the importance of following guidelines and behaving appropriately. However, it is equally important to enforce these boundaries with love and understanding. By taking the time to explain why certain behaviors are unacceptable and how they can make better choices in the future, we are teaching our children valuable lessons that will stay with them throughout their lives.

As fathers, we must also lead by example when it comes to discipline. Children learn by watching the adults in their lives, so it is essential that we model the behavior we want to see in them. By demonstrating self-control, patience, and respect in our own actions, we show our children how to handle difficult situations with grace and strength. This not only helps them understand the importance of discipline, but also teaches them how to navigate challenges with integrity and dignity.

Teaching values and morals is another important aspect of discipline that goes hand in hand with love and understanding. As fathers, we have the opportunity to instill in our children the importance of honesty, kindness, and empathy. By teaching them to treat others with respect and compassion, we are helping them develop a strong moral compass that will guide them in making ethical decisions throughout their lives. It is through these lessons that we can shape our children into caring and responsible individuals who contribute positively to society.

Becoming a Godly Father

In serving as role models for our children, we have the power to influence their behavior and attitudes in profound ways. By embodying the qualities of a godly father – patience, forgiveness, and unconditional love – we show our children what it means to be a person of integrity and character. Through our actions and words, we can inspire them to strive for excellence, to stand up for what is right, and to always seek the path of righteousness. By teaching discipline with love and understanding, we are not only shaping the future of our children, but also leaving a lasting legacy of grace and strength for generations to come.

Handling Challenges and Difficult Situations with Discipline

In the journey of fatherhood, there will inevitably be challenges and difficult situations that you will face. It is crucial to approach these obstacles with discipline and grace in order to navigate them effectively. By handling challenges with discipline, you can set a positive example for your children and teach them important life skills.

One key aspect of handling challenges with discipline is maintaining a calm and composed demeanor. When faced with a difficult situation, it can be easy to react emotionally or impulsively. However, by taking a step back and approaching the situation with a clear mind, you can make better decisions and set a positive example for your children. Remember that your children are always watching and learning from your actions.

Becoming a Godly Father

Discipline also involves setting boundaries and enforcing them consistently. By establishing clear rules and consequences for behavior, you can teach your children the importance of accountability and responsibility. Consistency is key when it comes to discipline, as it helps children understand the expectations and consequences of their actions. By enforcing boundaries with love and understanding, you can help your children grow into responsible and respectful individuals.

Ultimately, handling challenges and difficult situations with discipline is an essential part of embracing the role of a godly father. By approaching obstacles with grace and strength, you can set a positive example for your children and teach them important life lessons. Remember that fatherhood is a journey filled with ups and downs, but by facing challenges with discipline, you can navigate them with confidence and grace.

Becoming a Godly Father

Chapter 4: Fatherhood and Teaching Values and Morals

Instilling Values of Honesty, Respect, and Integrity

In the journey of fatherhood, it is crucial to instill values of honesty, respect, and integrity in our children. These values serve as the foundation for building strong character and developing a sense of moral responsibility. As men and fathers, it is our duty to lead by example and teach our children the importance of living a life guided by these principles.

Honesty is a value that forms the basis of trust in any relationship. As fathers, we must demonstrate the importance of being truthful and transparent in our actions and words. By showing our children the value of honesty, we are teaching them to be trustworthy individuals who can be relied upon in all aspects of life.

Respect is another essential value that must be instilled in our children from a young age. We must teach our children to respect themselves, others, and the world around them. By modeling respectful behavior and teaching our children to treat others with kindness and consideration, we are helping them develop into empathetic and compassionate individuals who contribute positively to society.

Becoming a Godly Father

Integrity is the cornerstone of moral character. It is the quality of being honest and having strong moral principles. As fathers, we must teach our children to always do the right thing, even when no one is watching. By instilling a sense of integrity in our children, we are guiding them to make ethical decisions and uphold their values in all aspects of life.

Teaching the Importance of Kindness and Compassion

Teaching the importance of kindness and compassion is a crucial aspect of being a godly father. As men, fathers, and parents, it is our responsibility to instill these values in our children from a young age. Kindness and compassion are essential virtues that not only make our children better individuals but also contribute to building a more compassionate and empathetic society.

One of the key ways to teach kindness and compassion to our children is by modeling these behaviors ourselves. Children learn by example, and as fathers, we must demonstrate acts of kindness and compassion in our daily interactions with others. Whether it is helping a neighbor in need, showing empathy towards others, or simply being courteous and respectful, our actions speak louder than words and leave a lasting impression on our children.

Becoming a Godly Father

Another important aspect of teaching kindness and compassion is through intentional conversations and discussions with our children. We can talk to them about the importance of treating others with kindness, showing empathy towards those who are less fortunate, and standing up against injustice and bullying. By engaging in meaningful conversations with our children, we can help them develop a deeper understanding of the value of kindness and compassion in their lives.

In addition to modeling and discussing the importance of kindness and compassion, we can also encourage our children to participate in acts of service and volunteer work. By engaging in activities that involve helping others, our children can experience firsthand the joy and fulfillment that comes from making a positive impact in the lives of others. Whether it is volunteering at a local shelter, participating in a charity event, or simply lending a helping hand to a friend in need, these experiences can help cultivate a heart of compassion and empathy in our children.

Ultimately, teaching the importance of kindness and compassion is a lifelong journey that requires patience, consistency, and dedication. As fathers and parents, we have the unique opportunity to shape and mold the hearts and minds of our children, guiding them towards becoming kind, compassionate, and empathetic individuals. By embracing our roles as godly fathers and serving as role models of kindness and compassion, we can help create a more loving and compassionate world for future generations to come.

Becoming a Godly Father

Leading by Example in Living Out Values and Morals

As men and fathers, it is crucial that we lead by example in living out values and morals in our everyday lives. Our children look to us as their role models, and it is our responsibility to show them what it means to live a life of integrity and honor. By embracing our roles as godly fathers, we have the opportunity to positively impact the lives of our children and instill in them the values and morals that will guide them throughout their lives.

Fatherhood is not just about providing for our children's physical needs; it is also about teaching them the importance of discipline and self-control. By setting boundaries and enforcing consequences for their actions, we are helping them develop the self-discipline needed to succeed in life. As fathers, we must be consistent in our discipline and always show love and understanding as we guide our children on the right path.

One of the most important roles we have as fathers is to teach our children values and morals that will shape their character and guide their decisions. We must lead by example by showing them what it means to be honest, compassionate, and respectful towards others. By instilling these values in our children, we are equipping them with the tools they need to navigate the complexities of the world with grace and integrity.

Becoming a Godly Father

Being a role model for our children is a privilege and a responsibility that should not be taken lightly. Our actions speak louder than words, and our children are always watching and learning from us. By living out our values and morals in our daily lives, we are showing our children what it means to be a person of integrity and honor. As fathers, we have the power to shape the future by being positive role models for our children.

Embracing the roles of a godly father means leading by example in living out values and morals. By demonstrating discipline, teaching values, and serving as role models for our children, we are shaping their character and guiding them towards a life of purpose and meaning. Let us strive to be the best fathers we can be, showing our children what it means to live a life of integrity and honor.

Attitude and Behaviors Fathers must Avoid

When dealing with their children, fathers (and parents in general) must be careful to avoid behaviors and attitudes that can harm their relationship with their children or negatively impact their children's development and well-being. Here are some key behaviors and attitudes that fathers should avoid:

1. Favoritism

Scriptural Reference: Genesis 37:3-4

Becoming a Godly Father

Example: Jacob showed favoritism towards Joseph by giving him a special coat, which led to jealousy and strife among his brothers.

Impact: Favoritism can create jealousy, resentment, and hostility among siblings, damaging family unity and individual self-esteem. This was what led to the brothers selling Joseph

Isaac and Rebecca also showed favoritism to their twins Esau and Jacob. The result was an intense hatred and persecution of Jacob by Esau.

Genesis 25:27–28 (KJV)

And the boys grew: and Esau was a cunning hunter, a man of the field; and Jacob was a plain man, dwelling in tents.

28 And Isaac loved Esau, because he did eat of his venison: but Rebekah loved Jacob.

2. Harshness and Over-Discipline

Ephesians 6:4 (KJV)

Fathers, do not provoke your children to anger, but bring them up in the discipline and instruction of the Lord.

Impact: Being overly harsh or excessively strict can lead to fear, anger, and bitterness in children. It can break their spirit and hinder healthy emotional and psychological development.

3. Neglect

1 Timothy 5:8 (KJV)

But if anyone does not provide for his relatives, and especially for members of his household, he has denied the faith and is worse than an unbeliever.

Impact: Neglecting the physical, emotional, and spiritual needs of children can lead to feelings of abandonment and insecurity. It can also negatively affect their development and future relationships.

4. Lack of Encouragement and Affirmation

Colossians 3:21 (KJV)

Fathers, do not embitter your children, or they will become discouraged.

Impact: Failing to encourage and affirm your children can result in low self-esteem and a lack of confidence. Children need positive reinforcement to thrive and grow in a healthy manner.

5. Unrealistic Expectations

- Impact: Setting unrealistic or unachievable standards can cause stress and feelings of inadequacy in children. They may feel they are constantly letting their parents down, leading to anxiety and low self-worth.

6. Hypocrisy and Lying

Matthew 23:3 (KJV)

So you must be careful to do everything they tell you. But do not do what they do, for they do not practice what they preach.

Impact: Children are quick to pick up on inconsistencies between what their parents say and do. This can lead to confusion, a lack of respect, and a weakened moral compass.

Fathers that tell lies on the phone, in front of their children are setting them up for similar behaviors when they grow up.

Becoming a Godly Father

7. Overindulgence

Impact: Providing everything a child wants without setting limits can lead to entitlement, lack of discipline, and poor coping skills. Children might struggle with entitlement and fail to develop a sense of responsibility.

Example of this are the children of Eli. Their dad permitted them to get away with bad behaviors which ruined their lives and both died prematurely.

8. Bad Habits (Smoking and drinking, use of illicit drugs)

Impact: Use of alcohol, cigarettes and drugs set the children up for similar habits. Some kids learnt how to smoke from their dads and later become drug addicts.

9. Criticism Without Constructive Feedback

Impact: Constant criticism without providing constructive feedback can diminish a child's self-esteem and motivation. Children need to know not only what they are doing wrong but also how to improve.

Becoming a Godly Father

Summary:

Effective parenting requires a balance of guidance, discipline, love, and support. Fathers should strive to:

- Show unconditional love and acceptance.

- Encourage open and honest communication.

- Provide consistent and fair discipline.

- Spend quality time with each child, fostering individual bonds.

- Model integrity, kindness, and godliness.

- Support and nurture their children's physical, emotional, and spiritual development.

By avoiding harmful behaviors like favoritism, harshness, neglect, and hypocrisy, fathers can build strong, healthy relationships with their children and positively influence their growth and development.

Becoming a Godly Father

Chapter 5: Fatherhood and Serving as a Role Model

Being a Positive Influence in Your Children's Lives

Being a positive influence in your children's lives is one of the most important aspects of fatherhood. As a father, you have the unique opportunity to shape and mold your children into the individuals they are meant to be. By embracing your role with grace and strength, you can set a positive example for your children and help them grow into responsible, compassionate adults.

Fathers as Positive Role Models

Fathers play a crucial role in shaping the lives of their children. As positive role models, they impart values, behaviors, and life skills that significantly influence their children's development. The impact of a father's presence and example is profound, affecting various aspects of a child's growth and future.

Let no man despise thy youth; but be thou an example of the believers, in word, in conversation, in charity, in spirit, in faith, in purity. 1 Timothy 4:12 (KJV)

Becoming a Godly Father

Here's an expanded look at the importance and influence of fathers as positive role models:

1. Instilling Values and Ethics

Positive role model fathers teach their children core values such as honesty, integrity, respect, and responsibility. By demonstrating these values in their own lives, fathers help children understand their importance and applicability. For instance, a father who consistently tells the truth and honors commitments shows his children the value of integrity and trustworthiness.

2. Building Confidence and Self-Esteem

Children look to their fathers for affirmation and validation. A father who encourages, supports, and celebrates his children's achievements helps build their confidence and self-esteem. By acknowledging their efforts and successes, fathers reinforce a positive self-image and instill a sense of worth in their children.

3. Teaching Life Skills

Fathers often impart practical life skills to their children, such as problem-solving, financial management, and basic household tasks.

Becoming a Godly Father

By involving their children in these activities and teaching them how to navigate daily challenges, fathers prepare them for independent and competent adulthood.

4. Modeling Healthy Relationships

The way a father interacts with his partner, family members, and others sets a template for how children will approach relationships. Fathers who show respect, empathy, and effective communication in their interactions teach their children the foundations of healthy and loving relationships. This modeling helps children develop their own social skills and understand the importance of treating others with kindness and respect.

5. Demonstrating Work Ethic and Perseverance

A father's approach to work and perseverance in the face of challenges can significantly influence his children's attitudes toward work and resilience. Fathers who exhibit a strong work ethic, dedication, and the ability to overcome obstacles teach their children the value of hard work and persistence. This lesson is crucial for children's academic, professional, and personal success.

6. Encouraging Emotional Intelligence

Fathers who are emotionally available and express their feelings openly help their children develop emotional intelligence. By showing that it's okay to feel and express a range of emotions, fathers teach their children how to handle their own emotions effectively. This emotional guidance helps children build emotional resilience and develop healthy coping mechanisms.

7. Promoting Physical and Mental Well-being

Fathers who prioritize their health and well-being set a positive example for their children. Engaging in regular physical activity, maintaining a balanced diet, and practicing self-care teach children the importance of looking after their own health. Additionally, fathers who seek help for mental health issues and discuss these openly help destigmatize mental health, encouraging children to do the same.

8. Fostering a Love for Learning

Fathers who demonstrate a curiosity for knowledge and a love for learning inspire their children to value education and intellectual growth. Whether it's through reading, exploring new hobbies, or continuous professional development, fathers who engage in lifelong learning encourage their children to adopt a similar mindset.

Becoming a Godly Father

9. Providing Stability and Security

A father's consistent presence and reliability provide a sense of stability and security for children. Knowing that they can depend on their father for support and guidance helps children feel safe and grounded. This stability is essential for children's emotional and psychological development.

10. Being Involved and Present

Active involvement in a child's life—attending school events, engaging in their interests, and spending quality time together—shows children that they are valued and loved. This involvement strengthens the father-child bond and reinforces the father's role as a supportive and engaged parent.

Fathers who serve as positive role models play a vital role in the holistic development of their children. By instilling values, teaching life skills, modeling healthy behaviors, and providing emotional support, they set the foundation for their children to grow into responsible, confident, and compassionate adults. The influence of a positive role model father extends beyond childhood, shaping the attitudes, behaviors, and success of their children throughout their lives. In essence, the role of a father as a positive role model is indispensable in nurturing the next generation and contributing to a healthy and thriving society.

Becoming a Godly Father

Furthermore, as a father, you serve as a role model for your children. Your actions and attitudes will greatly influence how your children view the world and themselves. By demonstrating love, kindness, and respect in your interactions with others, you can show your children how to treat others with dignity and compassion. Serving as a positive role model for your children will help them develop strong character and integrity, enabling them to make wise decisions and lead fulfilling lives.

There are several ways in which we can be a role model at different stages in a child's life. When the child starts to develop lasting memories, we are being watched and studied, whether we know it or not.

Preschool years : Be kind to people. Be kind to your spouse. Most young kids model what they see regularly at home. Show them how to clean up after them selves, how to use the bathroom respectfully, putting the toilet seat down after each use to be considerate of female users. Say "I love you" and return the same phrase when said to you. Hug them, kiss them so they get used to outward show of affection. Affirm them often and correct in love. Teach them to love God by taking them to worship with you regularly.

Becoming a Godly Father

Elementary years: Similar to the preschool years, teach them how to be organized. Teach them how to apologize sincerely by acknowledging your faults when you make a mistake. Teach them humility and how to reflect on what could be done differently by saying out loud "I should have ———-". Teach them gratitude by saying thank you for the little things. Teach them to be a gentleman by treating your wife respectfully and nice in front of your kids. Teach them how to pray and read the Bible by inviting them to devotion regularly or have them seat with you when you are reading your bible. Teach them how to trust God by sharing prayer points with them and sharing testimonies of what God did in your life.

Middle school/ high school: Similar to the earlier years. In addition, Teach them about kindness in relationships by sharing your life challenges and victories with them. Teach them the value of hard work by taking them to work with you one day. Help them obtain a summer job so they can value money.

Help them respect females by the way you honor your wife or their mother. Teach them holiness by sharing scripture and practical examples in your life Teach them that the bible is the source of multiple solutions by using it to answer questions they may have about life and spirituality Help them transition into being a man by affirming them when they make the effort even if it is not perfect.

Becoming a Godly Father

Talk to them as an adult not a child to facilitate the environment of receptive mentorship. This is the phase when many lose their kids because they have not created a good environment for dialogue, trust and connection for ongoing relationships beyond the teenage years.

College Age and pre professional years: Same as high school and critical if you still have the relationships.

Teach them how to make major decisions by talking through the processes involved and your thinking so they can see how you did it. What are the factors, the pros and cons. Do a lot of listening here instead of telling. How it was during your time may no longer be valid so you need to be mindful that what used to be a "con" may now be a non issue. Do more listening, affirming, consulting and less telling. They have to learn to make their own mistakes and trust that you will be there for them no matter what. Remember you have been teaching them how to live life according to God's word. Even though it may not seen like it. They were listening. Praise them when they get it right. Be gentle if they get it wrong. As them what they are learning when they make a mistake. Pray against any spirit of pride that will prevent them from learning and growing.

Becoming a Godly Father

Professional years/ married years: You are there as a consultant, listener, cheerleader and prayer warrior. Pray more and supervise less. Be there for them when they need you. Affirmation is still critically needed here. Otherwise, enjoy your life with your wife. If you happen to be living in the home with your kids and family, be respectful of boundaries and remember you are NOT in charge there. Have fun being a role model for your children and grand children.

In conclusion, being a positive influence in your children's lives is a sacred responsibility that comes with the role of fatherhood. By embracing your role with grace and strength, you can guide and support your children as they navigate the ups and downs of life. Through discipline, teaching values and morals, and serving as a positive role model, you can help your children grow into confident, compassionate individuals who make a positive impact on the world around them.

Demonstrating Strength and Integrity in Your Actions

As a father, it is also important to serve as a role model for your children. By demonstrating strength and integrity in your own actions, you can show your children what it means to be a man of character and integrity. Whether it is through your work ethic, your relationships with others, or your commitment to your faith, your children will look to you as an example of how to live a life of purpose and meaning.

Becoming a Godly Father

Demonstrating strength and integrity in your actions as a father is essential to fulfilling your role as a godly father. By being consistent in your discipline, teaching values and morals, and serving as a positive role model for your children, you can help them grow into the best versions of themselves. Remember, your actions speak louder than words, so strive to embody the qualities of strength and integrity in all that you do as a father.

Inspiring Your Children to Embrace Their Own Faith and Values

As a father, one of the most important roles you have is to inspire your children to embrace their own faith and values. It is essential to instill in them a strong foundation of beliefs that will guide them throughout their lives. By teaching them the importance of faith and values, you are shaping their character and helping them become the best version of themselves.

One way to inspire your children to embrace their faith and values is by leading by example. Show them through your actions and words what it means to live a life guided by faith and values. Attend religious services together, participate in family prayers, and engage in discussions about your beliefs. By being a role model for your children, you are showing them the importance of living a life that is rooted in faith and values.

Becoming a Godly Father

Example of Job as a Father of Faith

Job 1:5 offers a profound example of the diligence, care, and spiritual leadership that are the hallmarks of good fatherhood.

The verse reads: "And it was so, when the days of their feasting were gone about, that Job sent and sanctified them, and rose up early in the morning, and offered burnt offerings according to the number of them all: for Job said, It may be that my sons have sinned, and cursed God in their hearts. Thus did Job continually."

Several key lessons can be distilled from this verse:

1. Spiritual Vigilance
Job's actions demonstrate an acute awareness of his children's spiritual well-being. He made it a point to consider the state of their hearts and their relationship with God. From this, fathers can learn the importance of being vigilant about the spiritual health of their family. It's crucial to be attentive to the ways one's family members might drift and to take proactive steps to guide them back.

2. Regular Intercession
Job's commitment to offering burnt offerings on behalf of his children "continually" shows the importance of regular intercession. Fathers can take this as a call to consistently pray for their children, seeking God's protection, guidance, and blessings for them. Intercessory prayer is a powerful way in which fathers can actively participate in their children's spiritual journey.

Becoming a Godly Father

3. Early Morning Discipline: The verse notes that Job rose up early in the morning to perform his duties. This implies the value of discipline and making time for important spiritual practices daily. Fathers can learn to prioritize time for spiritual activities, setting an example of diligence and commitment.

4. Precaution and Proactivity: Job did not wait for evidence of his children's sin; he acted preemptively ("It may be that my sons have sinned"). This proactive approach teaches fathers to address potential issues before they manifest into larger problems. Fathers should cultivate an environment where moral and spiritual integrity is maintained proactively.

5. Personal Responsibility: Job took it upon himself to sanctify his children, reflecting a sense of personal responsibility for their spiritual well-being. Fathers can learn the importance of taking initiative in guiding and nurturing their children's spiritual lives rather than leaving it entirely to external institutions or influences.

6. Consistency: The verse ends with "Thus did Job continually," emphasizing consistency in one's actions. Fathers can learn that consistency in spiritual practices, teaching, and leading by example is vital for instilling strong values and faith in their children.

Becoming a Godly Father

Practical Applications for Fathers:

1. **Set a Routine for Family Prayer and Worship**: Having regular times for family devotion can set a strong spiritual foundation.

2. **Pray for Each Child Specifically**: Lift up each child's unique needs, struggles, and growth areas in prayer.

3. **Model Discipline and Commitment**: Show through your actions how important spiritual practices are.

4. **Engage in Open Dialogues About Faith**: Create a safe space for your children to discuss their faith, doubts, and questions.

5. **Teach by Example**: Demonstrating integrity, compassion, and faith in your daily life is a powerful teaching tool.

In summary, Job 1:5 teaches fathers to be diligent, prayerful, proactive, disciplined, responsible, and consistent in their approach to nurturing their children's spiritual lives. These principles, when applied, can help fathers lead their families with wisdom and grace.

Another way to inspire your children is to teach them the importance of discipline. Discipline is essential for instilling values and morals in children. Set clear boundaries and expectations for behavior, and be consistent in enforcing them. By teaching your children the importance of discipline, you are helping them develop self-control and self-discipline, which are essential qualities for living a life guided by faith and values.

Becoming a Godly Father

Teaching values and morals to your children is another important aspect of inspiring them to embrace their faith and values. Talk to them about the values that are important to your family, such as honesty, kindness, and compassion. Encourage them to think about their own values and how they can live their lives in accordance with them. By teaching your children the importance of values and morals, you are helping them develop a strong sense of right and wrong, which will guide them in making decisions throughout their lives.

Finally, serving as a role model for your children is crucial in inspiring them to embrace their faith and values. Show them what it means to live a life of integrity, compassion, and faith. Be there for them when they need guidance and support, and show them that you are always there to help them navigate life's challenges. By serving as a role model for your children, you are demonstrating the importance of living a life that is guided by faith and values, and inspiring them to do the same.

Chapter 6: Abusive Fathers

Men Who Beat Their Wives: A Deep Dive into the Impact on Family, Children, and Society

2 Timothy 2:24 (KJV)

And the servant of the Lord must not strive; but be gentle unto all men, apt to teach, patient,

Domestic violence, particularly men beating their wives, is a severe and pervasive issue with far-reaching consequences. It is a manifestation of control and power that undermines the safety, dignity, and well-being of the victims. The impact of such violence extends beyond the immediate harm to the wife, affecting the entire family, especially children, and reverberating through society at large.

The Impact on the Family

1. Physical and Emotional Trauma for the Wife

- **Physical Injuries**: Women who are subjected to domestic violence often suffer from a range of physical injuries, from bruises and cuts to broken bones and internal injuries. These physical traumas can have long-lasting health implications.
- **Emotional and Psychological Damage**: The emotional toll of living in fear and constant danger is profound. Victims of domestic violence frequently experience depression, anxiety, post-traumatic stress disorder (PTSD), and other mental health issues. The psychological scars often last longer than physical injuries.

2. Erosion of Trust and Safety

- **Loss of Trust**: A husband who beats his wife destroys the foundational trust in their relationship. This betrayal makes it challenging to maintain any semblance of a healthy partnership.
- **Sense of Safety**: The home, ideally a sanctuary, becomes a place of terror. The wife's constant fear and anxiety about future violence disrupts the peace and stability of the household.

3. Economic Consequences

- **Financial Dependence**: Many victims of domestic violence find themselves financially dependent on their abusers, which complicates efforts to leave the abusive situation. This dependency can trap women in a cycle of abuse.
- **Economic Hardship**: Medical bills, legal fees, and the potential loss of employment due to injuries or emotional distress can lead to significant financial strain on the family.

The Impact on Children

1. Emotional and Psychological Effects

- **Trauma and Anxiety**: Children who witness domestic violence often experience trauma and anxiety. The fear of violence and the stress of living in an unpredictable environment can lead to long-term psychological issues.
- **Developmental Problems**: Exposure to domestic violence can hinder children's emotional and cognitive development. They may struggle with concentration, academic performance, and social interactions.

2. Behavioral Issues

- **Aggression and Violence**: Children model the behavior they observe. A child who witnesses a father beating a mother may come to see violence as an acceptable way to resolve conflicts, potentially becoming violent themselves.
- **Withdrawal and Depression**: Conversely, some children might internalize their trauma, leading to withdrawal, depression, and other mental health issues.

3. Impaired Relationships

- **Distrust of Relationships**: Witnessing domestic violence can severely impact a child's ability to form healthy relationships in the future. They may struggle with trust, fear intimacy, or have skewed perceptions of what constitutes a healthy relationship.
- **Parent-Child Relationship**: The relationship between the abusive father and the children often deteriorates. Children may fear or resent their father, leading to strained or severed relationships.

Becoming a Godly Father

The Impact on Society

1. Perpetuation of Violence

- **Cycle of Abuse**: Children who grow up in violent households are more likely to perpetuate the cycle of abuse in their own relationships. This creates a generational pattern of violence that is difficult to break.
- **Normalization of Violence**: Widespread domestic violence can normalize abusive behavior in society, leading to higher tolerance and less intervention in abusive situations.

2. Economic Costs

- **Healthcare Costs**: The medical costs associated with treating victims of domestic violence are substantial. This includes emergency room visits, ongoing medical care, and mental health services.
- **Legal and Social Services**: The legal system, including law enforcement, courts, and social services, bears a significant burden in addressing and managing cases of domestic violence.

3. Loss of Productivity

Workplace Impact

Victims of domestic violence may have increased absenteeism, reduced productivity, and higher job turnover. This impacts businesses and the broader economy.

4. Community Health and Safety

- **Increased Crime Rates**: Domestic violence contributes to overall crime rates and can lead to other forms of violence and criminal behavior.
- **Community Well-being**: High rates of domestic violence can erode the sense of community well-being and safety, leading to social instability.

Addressing the Problem

1. Legal and Policy Measures

- **Protective Services**: Access to protective services such as shelters, hotlines, and legal aid is vital for victims seeking to escape abusive situations.

2. Education and Awareness

- **Public Awareness Campaigns**: Educating the public about the signs of domestic violence and how to help can reduce stigma and encourage intervention.
- **School Programs**: Implementing programs in schools to teach children about healthy relationships and conflict resolution can help break the cycle of violence.

3. Support Systems

- **Counseling and Support Groups**: Providing mental health support and counseling for both victims and perpetrators can help address the underlying issues and promote healing.
- **Economic Empowerment**: Programs that help victims gain financial independence, such as job training and financial literacy courses, can empower them to leave abusive relationships.

Becoming a Godly Father

4. Community Involvement

- **Community-Based Initiatives**: Grassroots movements and community organizations such as churches can play a crucial role in supporting victims, raising awareness, and advocating for policy changes.
- **Engagement of Men and Boys**: Encouraging men and boys to be allies in the fight against domestic violence and to challenge toxic masculinity can foster a culture of respect and equality.

Men who beat their wives inflict profound harm on their families, children, and society. The immediate physical and emotional damage to the wife is just the beginning. The negative impact extends to children, who suffer emotionally, psychologically, and behaviorally, and to society, which bears the economic and social costs of domestic violence. Addressing this issue requires a comprehensive approach, including legal measures, education, support systems, and community involvement. By fostering a culture that condemns violence and promotes healthy, respectful relationships, we can work towards a future where domestic violence is eradicated, and families can thrive in safe and supportive environments.

Treat Your Wife Right

How to treat your wife before your children (their mother)

Embracing Your Roles With Grace and Strength

Becoming a Godly Father

Children learn valuable lessons about raising good families when they see good examples in their own parents. How fathers treat their wives in front of their children has a profound impact not only on their marriage but also on their children's understanding of relationships, respect, and love. Acting as positive role models is crucial for raising well-balanced, respectful, and loving children.

Here are some proper ways men (fathers) should treat their wives in front of their children:

1. Respect Her

Demonstrating respect towards your wife sets a powerful example. Speak to her kindly and listen to her opinions without dismissiveness. Don't yell at her in front of the kids. Don't insult their mom or raise your hands on her.

Ephesians 5:33: "However, let each one of you love his wife as himself, and let the wife see that she respects her husband."

2. Love Her

Love is visible, not hidden. Love is action in motion. Your children can discern if you truly love their mother by your actions.

Becoming a Godly Father

Affection: Simple acts of affection like a hug, a kiss, or holding hands show children that love and physical affection are important parts of a healthy marriage.

Verbal Affirmation: Saying "I love you" and expressing appreciation for your wife in front of the children reinforces the importance of verbal expressions of love.

3. Communicate Positively and Constructively with Her

Healthy Communication: Engage in discussions and decision-making processes openly, listening actively, and responding considerately.

James 1:19: "Know this, my beloved brothers: let every person be quick to hear, slow to speak, slow to anger."

4. Display Partnership and Teamwork

Teamwork: Show that marriage is a partnership by sharing responsibilities and making joint decisions, demonstrating a united front.

Philippians 2:2: "Complete my joy by being of the same mind, having the same love, being in full accord and of one mind."

Becoming a Godly Father

5. Handle Disagreements with Maturity

Conflict Resolution: Disagreements are natural, but handling them with calmness, respect, and a willingness to understand each other is key. Avoid shouting, insults, or any form of disrespectful behavior.

Ephesians 4:26 KJV: *"In your anger do not sin": Do not let the sun go down while you are still angry."*

6. Demonstrate Patience and Forgiveness

Patience: Show patience in moments of stress or misunderstanding. This teaches children the value of being patient and forgiving in relationships.

Colossians 3:13 KJV: *"Bear with each other and forgive one another if any of you has a grievance against someone. Forgive as the Lord forgave you."*

7. Share Responsibilities

Household Chores: Share household responsibilities, showing that both partners contribute to the home equally. This fosters a sense of equality and teamwork.

Becoming a Godly Father

Galatians 6:2 KJV: *"Bear one another's burdens, and so fulfill the law of Christ."*

8. Support and Encourage

Encouragement: Regularly encourage and support your wife's endeavors, ambitions, and well-being. This teaches children the importance of being each other's cheerleaders.

1 Thessalonians 5:11 KJV: *"Therefore encourage one another and build one another up, just as you are doing."*

9. Demonstrate Humility and Repentance

Admit Mistakes: When appropriate, admit your mistakes in front of the children and show repentance. Apologize to your wife if needed. This teaches children accountability and humility.

James 5:16 KJV: *"Therefore, confess your sins to one another and pray for one another, that you may be healed. The prayer of a righteous person has great power as it is working."*

Becoming a Godly Father

10. Instill and Demonstrate Moral and Spiritual Values

Faith and Values: Uphold and practice your shared moral and spiritual values. Pray together and partake in spiritual activities as a family.

Proverbs 22:6 KJV*: "Train up a child in the way he should go; even when he is old he will not depart from it."*

By treating their wives with respect, love, patience, and support, fathers model the behavior they hope to see in their children. These actions build a strong, loving family environment and instill values that children will carry into their future relationships.

By adhering to these principles and reflecting biblical teachings in their behavior, fathers can foster a nurturing and positive family atmosphere, exemplifying the kind of love and respect that God intends for marital relationships.

Becoming a Godly Father

Abusive Fathers: Fathers Who Abuse Their Children

Abuse by fathers is a grave issue that affects millions of children worldwide. Abusive behavior can take many forms, including physical, emotional, psychological, and even sexual abuse. The effects of such abuse are profound and long-lasting, impacting not only the immediate victims but also the wider family and community. Understanding the nature of paternal abuse, its consequences, and the pathways to intervention and healing is crucial for addressing this pervasive problem.

Forms of Abuse by Fathers

1. Physical Abuse

- **Violence**: This includes hitting, slapping, punching, kicking, and using objects to cause harm. Physical abuse can result in visible injuries, such as bruises, cuts, and broken bones, as well as long-term physical health problems.
- **Physical Intimidation**: Fathers may use their physical presence or force to intimidate and control their children, instilling fear and submission.

2. Emotional and Psychological Abuse

- **Verbal Abuse**: Constant criticism, belittling, name-calling, and shouting are forms of verbal abuse that erode a child's self-esteem and sense of worth.
- **Manipulation and Gaslighting**: Abusive fathers may manipulate their children's perception of reality, making them doubt their own experiences and feelings.
- **Emotional Neglect**: Withholding affection, love, and emotional support can be as damaging as overt abuse, leading to feelings of isolation and worthlessness.

3. Sexual Abuse

- **Molestation and Rape**: This includes any non-consensual sexual contact or activity imposed by the father on the child. The trauma from such acts can cause severe psychological damage and long-term mental health issues.
- **Exploitation**: Abusive fathers may exploit their children for sexual purposes, including coercing them into pornography or prostitution.

4. Financial Abuse

- **Control of Resources**: Fathers may exert control over financial resources, limiting their children's access to money and financial independence.
- **Economic Exploitation**: Using a child's labor without fair compensation or exploiting their talents for personal gain.

Impact on Children and Families

1. Emotional and Psychological Damage

- **Mental Health Issues**: Children who experience abuse are at higher risk for mental health disorders such as depression, anxiety, PTSD, and suicidal tendencies.
- **Low Self-Esteem**: Constant criticism and belittling can lead to chronic low self-esteem and feelings of inadequacy.
- **Trust Issues**: Abused children often struggle to trust others, which can affect their ability to form healthy relationships later in life.

Becoming a Godly Father

2. Behavioral Problems

- **Aggression**: Exposure to violence can lead to aggressive behaviors in children, as they may mimic the abusive patterns they have observed.
- **Withdrawal**: Some children may become socially withdrawn and isolated as a coping mechanism to deal with their trauma.

3. Academic and Social Impacts

- **Poor Academic Performance**: The stress and instability caused by abuse can negatively impact a child's academic performance and concentration.
- **Social Difficulties**: Abused children may struggle with social interactions and building relationships with peers, often due to trust issues and low self-esteem.

4. Physical Health Issues

- **Injuries**: Physical abuse can result in immediate injuries and long-term physical health problems.

- **Chronic Health Problems**: The stress and trauma of abuse can lead to chronic health issues such as headaches, gastrointestinal problems, and sleep disorders.

5. Intergenerational Transmission of Abuse

Cycle of Abuse

Children who grow up in abusive environments are at higher risk of perpetuating the cycle of abuse in their own relationships and families.

Societal Impacts

1. Increased Healthcare Costs

- **Medical Treatment**: The physical and psychological injuries caused by abuse often require extensive medical and therapeutic interventions, increasing healthcare costs.
- **Mental Health Services**: There is a higher demand for mental health services to address the trauma and its long-term effects.

2. Social Services Burden

- **Child Protection Services**: Increased need for child protective services to intervene and provide safe environments for abused children.
- **Legal and Judicial Systems**: Higher demand on legal and judicial systems to handle cases of abuse and provide justice and protection for victims.

3. Economic Costs

- **Productivity Loss**: Abuse can lead to long-term mental and physical health problems that affect an individual's ability to work and contribute economically.
- **Social Welfare Programs**: Increased reliance on social welfare programs to support victims of abuse who may struggle with employment and financial independence.

Becoming a Godly Father

Pathways to Intervention and Healing

1. Recognizing and Acknowledging Abuse

- **Education and Awareness**: Raising awareness about the signs of abuse and its impacts is crucial for early recognition and intervention.
- **Breaking the Silence**: Encouraging open dialogue and providing safe spaces for victims to share their experiences without fear of judgment or retribution.

2. Seeking Professional Help

- **Therapy and Counseling**: Professional therapy and counseling can provide a safe space for victims to process their trauma and begin the healing process. Family therapy can also help address and resolve underlying issues.
- **Support Groups**: Joining support groups for abuse survivors can offer emotional support, understanding, and practical advice from others who have experienced similar situations.

3. Legal and Protective Measures

- **Restraining Orders**: Legal measures such as restraining orders can protect victims from further abuse. It's important to understand and utilize the legal resources available for protection.
- **Child Protective Services**: In cases where children are at risk, child protective services can intervene to ensure their safety and well-being.

4. Building a Support Network

- **Family and Friends**: A strong support network of family and friends can provide emotional and practical support for victims of abuse. Encouraging open communication and providing a safe space for sharing can make a significant difference.
- **Community Resources**: Utilizing community resources such as shelters, hotlines, and advocacy groups can provide additional support and resources for victims seeking to escape abusive situations.

Becoming a Godly Father

5. Empowerment and Independence

- **Financial Independence**: Helping victims achieve financial independence through job training, education, and financial literacy can empower them to leave abusive relationships.
- **Personal Empowerment**: Empowering victims to regain control over their lives through self-help strategies, confidence-building activities, and assertiveness training is crucial for their long-term well-being.

6. Preventative Measures and Education

- **Early Intervention**: Identifying and addressing abusive behavior early can prevent the escalation of abuse. Schools, healthcare providers, and community organizations can play a key role in early intervention.
- **Educational Programs**: Implementing educational programs that teach healthy relationship skills, conflict resolution, and emotional regulation can help prevent abuse and promote healthy family dynamics.

Becoming a Godly Father

Abusive fathers can inflict severe and lasting harm on their children and families, with effects that can ripple through society. Understanding the different forms of abuse and their profound impacts is essential for addressing and mitigating this issue. By recognizing abuse, seeking professional help, utilizing legal protections, and building strong support networks, families can work towards healing and recovery. Empowerment, education, and early intervention are crucial in breaking the cycle of abuse and fostering healthier, more supportive family environments. Addressing abusive behavior not only improves the lives of individual family members but also contributes to the overall health and stability of society.

Chapter 7: Reconciliation and Renewal: Fathers in Conflict with Their Children

Conflict between fathers and their children can arise from various sources, such as generational differences, miscommunication, unmet expectations, or deeper issues like addiction and abuse. These conflicts can lead to strained or broken relationships, affecting the emotional and psychological well-being of both the father and the children. However, reconciliation and renewal are possible, and when achieved, they can transform these relationships, fostering a sense of healing, understanding, and mutual respect.

The Prevalence of Conflict Between Fathers and Children

Conflict between fathers and their children is a common issue across various societies and cultures.

Conflicts between fathers and sons are particularly common, often stemming from the development of masculine ego as boys reach puberty. By the age of 17 or 18, a young man may be as tall as his father and possibly even outweigh him. This physical maturity can lead him to mistakenly believe he is ready to take charge, much like his father. Meanwhile, the father still sees his son as a child and continues to issue directives. This dynamic frequently results in a clash of authorities, as both struggle to assert their roles within the family.

Becoming a Godly Father

This prevalence of father- children conflict can be attributed to several factors, including generational differences, communication breakdowns, societal pressures, and personal issues. Understanding the scope and nature of these conflicts helps in addressing them effectively and working towards reconciliation and renewal.

While exact prevalence rates of father-child conflicts can vary widely, research and surveys provide some insights into how common these issues are:

1. Family Dynamics Surveys

Studies conducted by family dynamics researchers often reveal that a significant percentage of families experience some level of conflict between parents and children. For instance, a survey by the Pew Research Center found that around 60% of families reported experiencing regular conflicts between parents and their teenage children.

2. Mental Health Reports

Reports from mental health organizations indicate that familial conflict is a common issue among those seeking therapy or counseling. According to the American Psychological Association (APA), family-related stress, including conflict between fathers and children, is one of the top reasons individuals seek psychological help.

3. Educational Studies

Educational institutions frequently encounter issues stemming from family conflicts. Studies by the National Center for Education Statistics (NCES) show that students from homes with high levels of conflict tend to have lower academic performance and higher rates of behavioral problems.

4. Socioeconomic Impact Studies

Research on socioeconomic impacts highlights that father-child conflicts are prevalent across different socioeconomic groups. However, the nature and intensity of these conflicts can be influenced by factors such as economic stress, employment status, and access to resources.

Understanding the Roots of Conflict

1. Generational Differences

- **Values and Beliefs**: Generational gaps often lead to different values, beliefs, and worldviews. Fathers may hold traditional views, while their children may embrace more contemporary or progressive ideas, leading to misunderstandings and disagreements.

- **Communication Styles**: Different generations may have distinct communication styles, with fathers possibly favoring direct and authoritative communication, while children might prefer open and egalitarian dialogue.

2. Unmet Expectations

- **High Expectations**: Fathers may have high expectations regarding their children's academic, career, or personal lives. When children fail to meet these expectations, it can lead to disappointment and conflict.
- **Personal Aspirations**: Children might have aspirations and dreams that differ from their fathers' expectations, leading to clashes over choices related to education, career, or lifestyle. For example, a father wants his son to study law but the young man is tending towards theater arts! One of them has to yield, otherwise conflict becomes inevitable.

3. Behavioral and Lifestyle Issues

- **Addiction and Substance Abuse**: Issues such as addiction or substance abuse can create significant conflict, with fathers struggling to understand or manage their children's behaviors.

- **Rebellion and Independence**: Adolescents and young adults often seek independence, sometimes rebelling against parental authority. This quest for autonomy can lead to frequent conflicts.

4. Emotional and Psychological Factors

- **Past Trauma**: Unresolved past traumas or emotional wounds can resurface and cause ongoing tension between fathers and their children.
- **Mental Health Issues**: Mental health problems, whether in the father or the child, can exacerbate conflicts and make resolutions more challenging.

5. Disciplinary Disagreements

One of the most common sources of conflict is disagreements over discipline. Fathers may have strict disciplinary methods, while children may resist these approaches, leading to power struggles and arguments.

6. Emotional Distance

Emotional distance or lack of emotional connection can also be a source of conflict. Fathers who struggle to express their emotions or engage emotionally with their children may create a sense of detachment and misunderstanding.

Impact of Conflict

1. Emotional and Psychological Effects

Ongoing conflict between fathers and children can lead to emotional and psychological distress for both parties. Children may experience feelings of inadequacy, low self-esteem, and depression, while fathers may struggle with guilt, frustration, and helplessness.

2. Academic and Social Outcomes

Children from conflict-ridden homes often face academic challenges and social difficulties. The stress and instability at home can impact their concentration, behavior, and relationships with peers and teachers.

3. Family Cohesion

Becoming a Godly Father

Persistent conflict can erode family cohesion, leading to estrangement and breakdown of family relationships. The lack of a supportive and harmonious family environment can have long-lasting effects on all family members.

4. Intergenerational Effects

The impact of father-child conflicts can extend to future generations. Children who grow up in conflict-ridden homes may struggle with their own relationships and may perpetuate similar patterns of conflict with their children.

Steps Toward Reconciliation

1. Acknowledging the Conflict

- **Acceptance**: Both parties must acknowledge that there is a conflict. Denial or minimization of issues only prolongs the discord.
- **Understanding Impact**: Recognizing the emotional and psychological impact of the conflict on both sides is crucial for taking the first steps toward healing.

Becoming a Godly Father

2. Open Communication

- **Active Listening**: Fathers and children need to practice active listening, which involves truly hearing and understanding each other's perspectives without immediate judgment or interruption.
- **Expressing Feelings**: Both parties should feel safe to express their feelings, fears, and frustrations openly. This helps in uncovering the root causes of the conflict.

3. Seeking Common Ground

- **Shared Goals**: Identifying shared goals and values can provide a foundation for rebuilding the relationship. These could include mutual love, respect, and the desire for a harmonious family life.
- **Compromise**: Reconciliation often requires compromise from both sides. Understanding that no one has to be completely right or wrong can facilitate a more flexible approach to resolving issues.

4. Apologizing and Forgiving

Becoming a Godly Father

- **Sincere Apologies**: Offering a sincere apology for past actions that have caused pain is essential. This shows a willingness to take responsibility and make amends.

- **Forgiveness**: Forgiveness is a critical component of reconciliation. It allows both parties to let go of past grievances and move forward with a clean slate.

5. Professional Help

- **Therapy and Counseling**: Professional therapists or counselors can provide a neutral space for fathers and children to explore their issues and develop healthier communication patterns.

- **Support Groups**: Support groups for parents and children dealing with similar issues can offer valuable insights and encouragement.

6. Rebuilding Trust

- **Consistency**: Rebuilding trust takes time and consistency. Fathers and children must demonstrate reliable and predictable behaviors that reinforce trustworthiness.

Becoming a Godly Father

- **Positive Interactions**: Engaging in positive and constructive activities together can help rebuild trust and strengthen the bond.

The Process of Renewal

1. Establishing New Norms

- **New Communication Patterns**: Developing new, healthier communication patterns that are respectful and empathetic helps prevent future conflicts.
- **Redefined Roles**: As children grow and develop their own identities, fathers may need to redefine their roles, shifting from authoritative figures to supportive mentors.

2. Ongoing Support and Reinforcement

- **Continual Effort**: Reconciliation is not a one-time event but an ongoing process. Both parties must continually work on maintaining the renewed relationship.
- **Support Networks**: Leveraging support from extended family, friends, and community resources can provide additional reinforcement for the renewed relationship.

Becoming a Godly Father

3. Celebrating Progress

- **Acknowledging Milestones**: Celebrating small victories and milestones in the reconciliation process helps maintain momentum and provides encouragement.
- **Gratitude and Appreciation**: Regularly expressing gratitude and appreciation for each other's efforts reinforces positive behaviors and strengthens the bond.

Benefits of Reconciliation and Renewal

1. Emotional and Psychological Well-being

- **Healing**: Reconciliation can lead to emotional healing for both fathers and children, helping to resolve long-standing emotional wounds and traumas.
- **Mental Health**: Improved relationships contribute to better mental health, reducing stress, anxiety, and depression for both parties.

2. Stronger Family Bonds

- **Unity**: Reconciliation fosters a sense of unity and cohesion within the family, creating a supportive environment for all members.

Embracing Your Roles With Grace and Strength

Becoming a Godly Father

- **Support System**: A renewed father-child relationship enhances the overall family support system, providing a reliable network for dealing with future challenges.

3. Positive Role Modeling

- **Healthy Relationships**: Fathers who successfully reconcile with their children serve as positive role models, demonstrating the importance of resolving conflicts and maintaining healthy relationships.
- **Intergenerational Impact**: The benefits of reconciliation can extend to future generations, as children who experience and witness positive relationship dynamics are likely to replicate them in their own lives.

4. Community and Societal Impact

- **Stronger Communities**: Healthy family relationships contribute to stronger, more resilient communities. Families that support and nurture each other are better equipped to contribute positively to society.

Becoming a Godly Father

- **Reduction in Social Problems**: Reconciliation and renewal within families can help reduce social problems such as crime, substance abuse, and mental health issues, which are often linked to familial conflict and dysfunction.

Becoming a Godly Father

Chapter 8: Family and Relationships

There's so much to say about a godly father and his family and relationships. I will use the acronym **F.A.M.I.L.Y** to discuss this.

F.

"F" stands for first things first. God must be our number one. And the scripture that, emphasizes that is in

Deuteronomy 6:5 (KJV)

"*And thou shall love thy Lord thy God with all thine heart, and with all thy soul, and with all thy might*".

One of the things that is very important about the scripture verse is our heart. And sometimes when you think about the heart, you think about a house. If you own a house, the question is, "Where is God in your house?" Is he in the basement, garage, or bathroom? When we read "Thou shall love the lord thy God with all thy heart." That means every room, every corner, every single nook and cranny is permeated with the presence of God.

Becoming a Godly Father

What is the state of your heart? Where is God in your heart? It is not enough to just say, Lord, I give you my heart, but did you really give him your whole heart or have you given him your bathroom compartment in your heart? When we think of the heart, we are thinking of the things you spend your heart on, relationships, thoughts, beliefs, cultural practices. Is God permeating all those aspects of your life? It is a really good scripture verse and I encourage you to meditate on it. There's so much insight in those two verses.

First things first, must be God. Too many times, God is a consultant for us. You've made up your mind. You've prepared the proposal. You have your justification, then you bring it to God in prayer. Lord, I want you to stamp this. That's what most people do. It should be the other way around. What do you want Lord? What would you have me do, Lord? And then he will be the one that will tell you about how to write the justification, the proposal and everything on how to execute. That's how we need to run our lives. Everything you do must be out of purpose. We need to move by instruction. When God wants you to be in a place because he has destinies that are tied to you, then you say "yes Lord" to everything he asks you to do. God first.

Becoming a Godly Father

There are certain things that God has prepared you for that you may not even know why. But he knows why, and I want you to make sure that you are living a life of purpose. Things might seem random, casual, and you may ask, "how are we here?" You must believe that God has a purpose, and you must be connected to God and move by faith. "First things first" means God is number one, no compromises, you must be plugged in 100% into him. Then, if you're married, your wife comes next. If you have kids, then the kids' needs come after that,

Next, your vocation, then everybody else. Some of us have it the other way around. Everybody else first, and then God is the last thing. Or it's your job that is first, and then God is the last thing. Or in some cases, it is your kid that is first, and God is the last thing. We need to have the order and the priorities appropriate to keep the first thing first.

Deuteronomy 11:22-25 (KJV)

"For if ye shall diligently keep all these commandments which I command you, to do them, to love the LORD your God, to walk in all his ways, and to cleave unto him; Then will the LORD drive out all these nations from before you, and ye shall possess greater nations and mightier than yourselves.

Becoming a Godly Father

Every place whereon the soles of your feet shall tread shall be yours: from the wilderness and Lebanon, from the river, the river Euphrates, even unto the uttermost sea shall your coast be. There shall no man be able to stand before you: for the LORD your God shall lay the fear of you and the dread of you upon all the land that ye shall tread upon, as he hath said unto you."

It says, for if you will diligently keep all these commandments. Generally, we may think of commandments as 10 commandments, however, every instruction of God is a commandment. It's not a suggestion, consideration or idea. It is what He needs us to do. Therefore, we need to move according to the Holy Ghost. It says, all these commandments which I command you to do them, to love the Lord your God, to walk in his ways, and to cleave onto him. This means cleaving onto your first marriage with God. How good is your marriage with God? "Then will the Lord drive out all these nations from before you".

You know, sometimes we are good prayer warriors, but we don't follow the instruction provided before the "then". We are asking for what comes after the "then" before we do what we should do before earning what comes after "then". God has given us the answer, the solution to the quiz, the solution to the problem.

The verse reads "*If you will diligently keep all these commandments,*" so just follow instructions provided, to love the Lord your God, to walk in his ways. You make up your mind.

Becoming a Godly Father

This is the first thing, "F". The first thing I'm going to do is to cleave onto him, making sure that your first marriage is with God. He said, "*then the Lord will drive out all these nations from before you*". You don't even have to ask for it. It will be an automatic occurrence, "*and you will possess greater nations and mightier than yourself.*" So, wealth will come your way. Why? Because you made the first thing the first thing. But many times, we make the last thing the first thing. We're pursuing the wealth, and God is saying, look. That thing you're looking for is in Me. Come to Me, I will give you all those things when you make the First thing first.

He says "*everywhere, the sole of your feet will tread will become yours*". You walk into a committee, you walk into an office, they see you smile, they say, "I want that person on my team". Before you know it, everybody wants you on their team. Why? Because you know what the first thing is. The verse references territory. He will expand the territory for you.

"*There shall no man be able to stand before you.*"
You won't have to be afraid. Everybody has fears, but you won't have to be afraid. Why? Because God is going to be like the Goliaths for them, even though He is bigger than Goliath. Many times, we feel like the David, and there's this Goliath, whatever it is, career, job, loan, whatever it is that is looming over you, and you're intimidated by. God says, you don't even need to worry. Do that thing first, then all the other things will start happening.

Becoming a Godly Father

Ther is a lot to learn here. When the Holy Ghost revealed this to me several years ago, I was inspired. This is where it's at. If you don't remember anything, remember this one. First things first. Love the Lord your God with all your heart, with all your soul, with all your mind, essentially, your everything. He must be your number one.

A.

A is for accountability. Keep your promises.

I remember a story about one of my uncles when I was little. He made lots of promises. We need to be careful with promises, particularly when you're dealing with young people. Also, if you are married and you're promising your wife, hey. I will do this because you want to shut her up. It's not going to help you later, don't tell her lies.

It helps you build trust when you are accountable. Look at James 5:12,

James 5:12 (KJV)
"*But above all things, my brethren, swear not, neither by heaven, neither by the earth, neither by any other oath: but let your yea be yea; and your nay, nay; lest ye fall into condemnation.*"

Becoming a Godly Father

Let me tell you a story about my uncle. The one I remember the most is one day he said that he was going to take us to the pool. He had made that promise so many times, and this day was going to be the day when we believed it would happen. My self and my siblings were ready. We were packed up, you know, like young kids, about 7, 8, years of age. We had our flip flops, swimsuits, towels and other things. We stood, and we waited, and we waited believing he would come soon.

I think he may have finally shown up at some point, and then he had some kind of excuse, but that pool visit was not going to happen anymore. From that moment in time, anytime he would say something, we knew he didn't mean what he was saying. You just smile and keep going.

Do our spouses believe us? When you make promises to your kids or grandkids, or workmates, do they believe you? This habit or behavior follows you wherever you go.

For example, you promise "I will have it to you by tonight." Suddenly it is 11:59pm, 30 seconds, and the person who you made the promise to is trusting God whether they are going to send it at the final second of the day. Unfortunately, it doesn't happen and somehow it doesn't bother you. You didn't even apologize. You didn't even acknowledge the occurrence. You were quick to find an excuse. What was due on that day became 10 days later before you even thought to bring it up. We must watch that. Accountability is critical.

Becoming a Godly Father

If you find that people don't trust you, and they're looking at you, and you're angry at your spouse because they're disrespecting you, it might be this accountability issue. Do you say what you mean? Do you mean what you say? Don't make promises you can't keep. Because the moment it is looking like maybe you're not going to deliver on the promise, you start getting questions. "Did you send that thing?"

Unfortunately, that is why some people call their bosses micromanagers. However, you must ask the question, why are they micromanaging you? Maybe you are not accountable because your yes is not your yes. Your nay is not your nay. You promised to send it by 2 PM. When in fact you plan to send it next week at 2 PM. So, your boss will double-check. "Have you sent it? Copy me, please." People are double checking to make sure you're doing what you're supposed to be doing because of your track record of poor accountability.

Someone said, "I will send grandma money tomorrow." Did you send the money? When did you really send it? Grandma needed it yesterday. You haven't sent it today. Accountability. The school fees or tuition bill needed to be paid. That insurance needed to be renewed. You couldn't handle it, and then they came to foreclose your house, or your kid was kicked out of school.

Becoming a Godly Father

Accountability – Can people find you where you say you are? You say, "I'm going to the store", however, you went to see your best friend, or you went to watch a movie or you went to watch a game or something else. They can't find you wherever you say you went originally.

Keep your promises. Keep your word. It helps you build trust. Next letter is "M"

M.

On behalf of all our sisters. "M" is manage your mom.

Manage your mom. Remember we're talking about the heart, and we're using the, example of, the house. Right? Now it's interesting because the scripture is very clear,

Ephesians 6:2-3 (KJV)
"Honour thy father and mother; (which is the first commandment with promise;). That it may be well with thee, and thou mayest live long on the earth."

Exodus 20:12 (KJV)
"Honour thy father and thy mother: that thy days may be long upon the land which the LORD thy God giveth thee.'

Becoming a Godly Father

Here is another scripture that is important for you to follow.

1 Peter 3:7 (KJV)
"Likewise, ye husbands, dwell with them according to knowledge, giving honour unto the wife, as unto the weaker vessel, and as being heirs together of the grace of life; that your prayers be not hindered."

Maybe you've been praying some prayers, and they have not been answered. It might be that you're in violation of this scripture. In case you think your job is just to honor your mom, you must consider that if you honor your mom, your days are long. But what's the point of having long days without prayers answered?

I want you to have both. How about you? Have long days and have prayers answered. 1Peter 3:7 is worthy of memorization. God is saying, if you don't honor this woman, your prayers will not be answered. That's why this scripture is worthy of memorization. So how are you going to manage the mom, and manage your wife together?

Let us think about the analogy of your heart and that house again. Imagine the biggest house you've dreamed of since you were young. Who is living in the biggest room? Who is living in the biggest room? We call it master bedroom or owner's suite. It should be the Husband and wife. Both of you own the biggest room in the house.

Becoming a Godly Father

The assumption is that this is a household where God is in every nook and cranny. He's everywhere in that house. You've given him permission to permeate every space in that house.

Now there are other rooms in that house. Can you sleep in every room in that house at the same time? Not Possible. So, when scripture says, "*honor your wife*", you must give her the best of the spot. Does that mean when grandma comes to visit that she won't be taken care of? Of course not. There are other good rooms in the house. You assign her a suitable room for her to feel comfortable. However, the owner's suite is still reserved for you and your wife.

You must understand that in your heart, you will always have space for your mom. Additionally, make sure it's not the owner's suite that you have her in. If at any point in time your behavior is suggesting that you are living with your mom in the owner's suite meant for you and your wife, there's a problem. Furthermore, it is when those kinds of behaviors manifest, that your wife begins to act "weird" because she feels uncomfortable in her own home.

Therefore, if you notice that your wife is acting differently, you must double check what the issue is. Ask yourself "Where is grandma in this situation? am I giving her my owner's suite portion of my heart?" "Is it my wife that is with me in the Owner's suite/master bedroom?" That means your secrets, the conversations, the pillow talk, the listening should be between you and your wife. But when you start sharing secrets that should be shared with your wife and with your mom, you've crossed the line and given out your owner's suite.

<u>Embracing Your Roles With Grace and Strength</u>

Becoming a Godly Father

How to manage your Mom

The easy way to remember how to manage your mum is to use your ABCs.

A

"A" stands for appreciation. Appreciate grandma to the hilt. Grandma needs your love. I hope that my sons will continue to honor me when I grow old and they have their own wife, but I do not want them to replace me for the spot that their wife should have. There is a way you can honor your mom so much that she won't even need to wonder what's happening in the master bedroom. But if you don't do that appreciation work well enough it could be problematic. Let the grandkids help you if you have kids. Look for a way to honor grandma so much that she will be sending praises continually to you and your wife. Involve your wife in honoring your mom.

If it is a gift that needs to be received, plan it together and make room for spontaneous giving. He makes the connection with my people. For me and his folks, I show them love as well. Make sure that there's that crisscrossing of love. Make it such that there is no way to discriminate. If you've done your job well, your mom should love your wife more than you.

Embracing Your Roles With Grace and Strength

Becoming a Godly Father

When you feel a hint of jealousy when grandma and your wife are talking, then you've done a good job. If you are not at that level, then you have to work hard to get to that level. Make sure your wife does not ever feel like she is not in the owner's suite/master bedroom because your mum and your wife should not be rivals. They're not the same age. They're not in the same status. They should occupy different love rooms in your heart. Therefore, they don't need to be competing for the same bed. But when you start seeing that competition for your attention, then you have done something wrong. Therefore, you must remember your ABCs. Appreciate your mom.

B

Boundaries. Keep boundaries clear. There are some places that are out of bounds. Nobody should feel comfortable coming into your master bedroom other than you and your wife. And if you permit your kids, they should knock before coming in. If the boundaries don't exist, people will cross them if you don't help them understand. Therefore, set expectations and set boundaries.

To avoid confusion, and misunderstanding, agree upon them before a visit. For example, she should not be judging your wife's cooking. You knew her cooking status before you married her. Why are you allowing your mom's comments to affect your relationship with your wife? Boundaries. What is her business with that? You chose this woman for a reason You're supposed to protect your wife.

Becoming a Godly Father

C

The "C" is for several things: commit, communicate, correct where necessary. You should have courage enough to talk to grandma and say, "No" or "That's not how we operate in this house." So, if you keep grandma in the space of the house where she needs and she has the proper communication and you set expectations, hopefully you can keep everyone at peace. Sample phrases include: "this is what we do now that I'm married." "This is how we agreed to do things now".

I had to set expectations when my mom came to visit us. My husband and I had a conversation about how things are going to be and we executed the plan together. Thank goodness my mom is a woman of dignity. She doesn't overstep her bounds. For your mum, you may have to make time to sit down and to have a conversation without disrespecting her, appreciate her properly, make sure she's properly taken care of, but she must not cross the boundary and begin to share a bed with you and your wife in your heart.

Becoming a Godly Father

Also, as you manage your mom, make sure she is comfortable. Perhaps she's lost her husband. Look for ways to create connections for her friends. Keep her busy. There might be a project she can do. Women are not, frail like we think. Some of our grandmas in the church are leading bible study. Keep mom busy. Consider that when somebody has to teach the scripture and lead prayer on a regular basis and they have to prepare for the session and the message, they won't likely have time to be checking on what's in the pot or what did Jane say to me today. Keep them busy and connected. Give them a project to do that aligns with their strengths.

Because they're mature and seasoned in age, doesn't mean they're not capable. They're very sharp. I'm so impressed with the grandmas that are at our church. We're so grateful to God for the wisdom he gave us to engage them in 50 plus, to engage them in grandparents' work, and to engage them in mentoring other people. Let's do that for our moms. Make sure that they are busy. Create memories together. Use this time to listen, to learn from them, know about their culture, cover them, commit, help them feel reassured that they are not in competition with your wife. You can do it.

If you have lost your mom at one point in time, whoever is the predominant female in your life that could potentially be a threat to your wife must be managed with the ABCs.

Becoming a Godly Father

Next is "I"

I.

"I" points to you. You are the I in family. Because we need you here. You are the designated leader, so you must develop yourself because the success of your family and your relationships is heavily dependent on how you've developed yourself. Who do you need to be to become successful in family and relationships? Are you secure in yourself, or are you competing with your wife?

For example, she got promoted at work. Do you have to be promoted at your own work too. She is a part of the team, so whatever happens, you're going to get glory in the end. Be secure in yourself. Be humble. You are fighting spirits, not the people around you or the stories you are telling yourself. What story are you telling yourself?

Are you saying to yourself "Oh, she's earning a little bit more money now. She's going to be acting unkind to me. I'm going to have to put some laws down here so that she knows who's really wearing the pants in the house." Meanwhile, you didn't know that this woman has had a covenant with God from Proverbs

Proverbs 31:12 (KJV)
"She will do him good and not evil all the days of her life."

Becoming a Godly Father

Some of you may not know the covenant your wife has made with God, but you are interacting with them as if they are regular human beings, and you don't know that God has her in a very special place because of the covenant. She may be telling herself: "I am committed to this man. I'm going to serve him no matter what my portfolio looks like." And then you come and start treating her like she's an ordinary female. God will deal with such a man in such a way that he will be begging for mercy. Be secure in yourself.

You are fighting spirits not the people around you or the stories you are telling yourself. Whatever story you told yourself, "I don't want to support her to go to this job" because you have made up your mind regarding what's going to happen if she takes that job. Whereas, you didn't know that it was God that is trying to answer the prayer that you've been praying so that she can be a helper of your destiny.

Therefore, cast out demons not people. Whatever issue is happening in your life, cast out those demons so they do not ruin your marriage. If you don't know how, see your pastor, submit to deliverance. Sort out those behaviors that have been passed down from our dads, grandpas that are influencing our lives. Behaviors and patterns from parents, moms, mom's side, dad's side manifesting in your own life. Whenever you don't know why you are doing what you're doing, it could be a demonic spirit that needs to be cast out.

Becoming a Godly Father

2 Corinthians 10:3-6 (KJV)

"For though we walk in the flesh, we do not war after the flesh: (For the weapons of our warfare are not carnal, but mighty through God to the pulling down of strong holds;) Casting down imaginations, and every high thing that exalteth itself against the knowledge of God, and bringing into captivity every thought to the obedience of Christ; And having in a readiness to revenge all disobedience, when your obedience is fulfilled."

You need to cancel and remove whatsoever lineage, demon spirit that has been trying to control you, and it's constantly showing up. Triggers here and there, and it just manifests, and you're wondering, why. We can go through a deliverance process.

1 Peter 5:8-10 (KJV)

"Be sober, be vigilant; because your adversary the devil, as a roaring lion, walketh about, seeking whom he may devour: Whom resist stedfast in the faith, knowing that the same afflictions are accomplished in your brethren that are in the world. But the God of all grace, who hath called us unto his eternal glory by Christ Jesus, after that ye have suffered a while, make you perfect, stablish, strengthen, settle you."

Becoming a Godly Father

We also need to manage perceptions. People have perceptions about your home. They don't know what's really happening in your home. If you believe what they are saying or insinuating, it could create a rift between you and your wife. Remember, they weren't there when you were having that private conversation, manage that perception.

Develop yourself. Take courage and don't let somebody's view cloud the beauty and the joy you have in your home. Develop yourself. Choose the culture of heaven. You can't please everyone. What you agree to in your home is what you should do. What works in someone else's home may not work in yours.

As you develop yourself, remember who you are:

1 Peter 2:9 (KJV)
"But ye are a chosen generation, a royal priesthood, an holy nation, a peculiar people; that ye should shew forth the praises of him who hath called you out of darkness into his marvellous light:"

Therefore, don't let someone else's philosophy or what you read in a book or saw in a movie change who you are to your family. You need to be a chosen generation or royal priesthood. Be the king in your home. Be gracious and kind, not a brute or dictator. You are a Kingdom Man. Be like Jesus who is gracious, kind, accommodating, and patient. Let the entire 1 Corinthians 13, love chapter be who you are.

Becoming a Godly Father

"I" is developing yourself. Next is "L".

L.

L is lead by example. Now you are all developed man who has received the presence of the highest, and you really manifest accordingly, as a royal priesthood in your home, it is important that you lead in prayer. Some people think that "if I can't lead prayer for 1 hour, I am useless", and therefore, you avoid prayer like the plague. Don't be that person. Lead by example. A 30 second prayer is also powerful when prayed in agreement.

Do you know that the most powerful prayers are the ones that you pray with your wife? Did you know that a prayer of agreement is very powerful? That is why the enemy doesn't like marriage. Look at how many prayers are not happening because of divorce or anger or, sleeping in sperate bedrooms. Thank goodness for FaceTime. It doesn't matter if you are in Sidney, you can pray together. Five seconds happens fast. Whether you are in the car or about to drop people off. You can pray a quick prayer and be done. While praying longer is great, ideal and desirable, don't make perfect the enemy of good.

"We haven't prayed all day". Don't stress over it. Let's pray now. Hold her hand. Pray a quick prayer, then go to bed. You're good. You wake up in the morning, pray. Perhaps you didn't pray last week. You remember right there and then, then invite your wife and pray together.

<u>Embracing Your Roles With Grace and Strength</u>

Becoming a Godly Father

What is the best time to pray for your wife? If she is telling you stories about what happened at work and so on, don't interrupt her. Let her finish. When she's done, give her affirmation then pray together. Some example phrases include: "I am proud of you." "I know you got this." then pray together.
If you were feeling afraid or anxious when she was talking to you, that is a sign that you should come against the spirit of fear. Pray as if you were praying for yourself. Encourage her at the end. Tell her "All is going to be well in Jesus Name" or something like that. Leave it in the hands of God. You're the head of the house. You don't have to have a solution to every problem. That is God's job, not yours.

Some of the best prayers over my life happened form my husband and I am grateful to God that he takes the time to declare over my life. Do the same for your wife. She will love you for it. The things that you need to happen in the life and career or health of your wife, declare it. Say "I declare it in the name of Jesus". Send it as a text if you don't know how to really declare and you are trying to decide. She will appreciate the thoughtful gesture because the prayer that comes from you is powerful.
Just like her dad, you are next like how you value your mom. Therefore, you must really think about the words that are coming out of your mouth and make sure that you are declaring positive things.
Lead by example. Live, love, laugh, learn. Those are additional "L"s.

Becoming a Godly Father

When you laugh and love, you are creating memories. When you laugh, people remember. You may not know how much you're creating memories, but you are. When you're goofing off on the basketball court with your son or daughter or playing, or even when they are laughing at you that you didn't do it well, don't worry. That's creating memories for them. They are having fun. You don't have to be perfect to be a father. You just have to be there. Just be there.

As you show them love, there are some words that are powerful for your kids. They need to hear it from you. They hear from some of their teachers. They need to hear " I love you." "I am proud of you." "Great job." "Wow." "You did that." There is a whole list of affirmative words that you can share with your kids. Find 5 and use it frequently to show love to them.

Another way to show love and affirmation is to stand and clap or cheer when they are being recognized or when they do something special. Let them see you there clapping. Everybody may not be clapping, make sure you're clapping. They see you and register that my father will appreciate what I'm doing. You send a message that "I'm here." "I matter." "I am important." It goes a very long way for your kids.

Becoming a Godly Father

Affirm your kids. If you didn't affirm them before, start now. It doesn't matter whether they're 60 or 40, 30, 20, 12 or 5. They need your affirmation. It is powerful coming from a parent. They long for it and are trying to get your affirmation while they're doing everything they're doing. And then when they finally get it, they suddenly feel like they passed an exam. It's such a relief.

Therefore, please affirm your kids. Create memories. Go for vacation. It doesn't have to be in a faraway place or too expensive. Go to the next city over. Do something fun, somewhere different. Consider a one-day retreat, something that is not too expensive, perhaps one night. Make it fun. Just be together and create memories. Thank goodness for our phones. It sends you memories periodically and you can create a group chat for the family, you know, so that we can communicate with ourselves because everybody's in different places. You must communicate intentionally. Lead by example.

My husband will send us a photo from years ago, and we will laugh. Who's that? When was this? And it brings back positive memories. Take them on vacation or to the park or museum. Take them to watch the planes taking off. It's being together that they remember. I still remember how intentional my dad was when reading to us.

Becoming a Godly Father

My sister and I were reminiscing on this even though we have grown kids of our own and dad had already gone to be with the Lord almost 10 years prior. We still remembered that. We laughed together again creating another fresh memory. Create memories. Be goofy with your kids. Make them laugh. They remember.

Psalm 126:1-3 (KJV)

"When the LORD turned again the captivity of Zion, we were like them that dream. Then was our mouth filled with laughter, and our tongue with singing: then said they among the heathen, The LORD hath done great things for them. The LORD hath done great things for us; whereof we are glad."

Another way to create memories is to share testimonies and rejoice together. Do you dance with your kids when there is a testimony? It is important for us to pray with them. If they have an exam, pray with them. Something significant is happening, good or bad, pray with them. It doesn't matter if it is the same prayer, you prayed last week. The thought counts a great deal. This way they know you are thinking of them, and you care about what is transpiring in their lives.

Many times, I call to pray with my kids. If they can't pick up the phone, I put the prayer in the chat so they can read the prayer, so they know I'm thinking of them or I leave a prayer message.

Becoming a Godly Father

No matter what time of day or night it is, I put it in there so that they know I'm thinking of them. Then when they come back with the outcome or testimonies, then we are dancing and giving God thanks. As your kids what they want you to pray for. They will remember I was afraid, we prayed, God answered our prayer, and we rejoiced. Help them understand that cycle. That's how you teach them the cycle of appreciating God for what he has done.

So, it's not only prayer requests, but praise reports are important too. Help your kids understand, it is God who answered our prayers and we want to show our gratitude by praise, therefore we are going to rejoice together. I do the same thing with my spiritual children. Therefore, since you are the leader, lead by example. Help them understand that cycle. This is why we are singing. God has done great things for us.

Proverbs 17:22 (KJV)
"A merry heart doeth good like a medicine: but a broken spirit drieth the bones."

So, think about laughter as medicine, think about good times as medicine. It will carry you through those times when things are rough and tough, and then create a sunshine folder.

Becoming a Godly Father

Financial health: The church or your workplace has many financial experts that can consult for you. You should have a retirement plan and life insurance (with your wife as beneficiary and your kid(s) as contingent).

To summarize and as we think of a godly father in family and relationships, we must consider the following:

F.A.M.I.L.Y.

First things first. God must be our number one.

Accountability

Manage your Mom

"I" is developing yourself.

Lead by example

Your health is important

Becoming a Godly Father

We all need a sunshine folder. It's like your stress toolkit. What is it that people have said to you that have really encouraged you, memories, laughter, joyful occasions, pictures etc.? Put it in a little folder on your phone or somewhere where you can go back and read it so that way you can be encouraged by the Lord.

The last letter is "Y"

Y.

Y is "Your health". Your health is important.

3 John 1:2 (KJV)
"Beloved, I wish above all things that thou mayest prosper and be in health, even as thy soul prospereth."

Your physical health requires attending your annual checkup consistently. Care for yourself. Your family needs you to last as long as possible. So, if you have not scheduled your physical. Today is a good day to start the process. Many diseases are preventable if picked up during annual checkups.

Spiritual health is important too as you make the first thing the first thing. For mental health, make sure you have godly friends around you that are speaking positive things into your life.

Becoming a Godly Father

Dr. Alfred Bisi Tofade is a faith leader, a mentor, instructor, and a public speaker. He is a gifted teacher and a dynamic speaker. He has great passion for marriage, relationships, and leadership.

Dr. Toyin Tofade, a professor of pharmacy, an higher education administrator and a certified professional Co active Coach is a dynamic teacher, leader, mentor and prayer warrior.

Dr. Bisi and Toyin jointly wrote a book on marriage titled "Practical Outlines for Success in Marriage" in 2015, then 'The Kingdom Wife' in 2023 . They have been married for 26 years and are blessed with two wonderful boys.

Made in the USA
Columbia, SC
11 August 2024